PRAISE FOR BEYOND CHAMPIONSHIPS

Coach Dru has shared some valuable principles in life with us in *Beyond Championships*. My son, Jibri, came to Coach Dru's program at St. Vincent-St. Mary as a junior in high school and has become a better person and a better player. I am grateful for Coach Dru's mentoring and the leadership he is providing for so many young people. *Beyond Championships* reveals the heart and soul of a good man and a good coach. It's a must-read for young people, as well as for older people. Thanks, Coach Dru, for sharing with us some lifetime lessons we can all use on our journey.

Mel Blount, four-time Super Bowl champ and member of the NFL Hall of Fame

After graduating from high school, the number one question I received was, "What was it like playing with LeBron?" The second most-asked question was, "What kind of coach did you have?" The first question was easier to answer than the second. But now you can read this book and begin to understand how great a man Coach Dru is! For Coach Dru, living a full and productive life has always been about more than just basketball. It's about relationships and being a Christian man and being a great father. It's about how to treat women, how to compete, how to be a student athlete, and so much more. Coach Dru is the best coach I've ever had. Not just because he's so good at the X's and O's, but also because he knows how to help a young person be the best person he can be. Coach often asked, "Are you prepared for the game of life? Because it never stops, even when the clock on the scoreboard hits 00:00!" Thank you, Coach Dru, for all you have done to prepare me for the game of life.

Willie McGee, "Fab Five" member of the St. Vincent-St. Mary basketball team (1999–2003) and current assistant coach of the Chowan University men's basketball team

One of my favorite maxims is "serve the underserved," and few people put these words into practice like Coach Dru Joyce does. We all know the incredible work he did in helping LeBron James develop into the player and, more importantly, the individual he's become. I'm excited that in *Beyond Championships*, Coach Dru shares the principles that helped mold so many other young lives as well. Coach Dru's story should inspire all readers, both young and old alike, to have the faith to chase their dreams, no matter what obstacles they perceive to be in front of them.

> *Russell Simmons, cofounder of Def Jam Records and*
> *author of* Super Rich: A Guide to Having It All

Anything that Dru Joyce has to say is important, because he is a quality man who cares about young men!

> *Bishop F. Josephus Johnson II, presiding bishop*
> *of The Beth-El Fellowship of Visionary Churches*
> *and senior pastor of The House of the Lord*

Coach Dru's teachings on faith, family, and character are an inspiration to athletes and nonathletes alike. *Beyond Championships* transcends sports the way Coach Dru's influence on young lives reaches far beyond the basketball court.

> *Kristopher Belman, writer/director of the documentary*
> More Than a Game

Dad, you have been an ongoing leader in my life. I value what you taught me both on and away from the basketball court. You're a man of many quotes to live by. Each morning as I was growing up, you would always remind me, "Be a leader and not a follower today." Well, I would follow your lead any day. Proud to be a former player, a student to your lessons, and, most of all, I am proud to call you my dad.

> Dru Joyce III, "Fab Five" member of the St. Vincent-
> St. Mary basketball team (1999–2003)

Beyond Championships is what happens when one of the nation's most influential high school coaches lets us in on his secrets to success. Whether or not you love sports, this book and the life lessons herein are invaluable to both young and old. Sit down, read, enjoy, and learn!

> Harvey Mason Jr., music/movie producer; producer
> of More Than a Game

Heartfelt and inspiring, *Beyond Championships* is a book for people of all ages and both genders. The teachings from my father—Coach Dru— apply not only to sports but to life as well, and that's what makes this book so good. Through sports, we're able to see real-life situations and how they tie in both positively and negatively in our lives.

> Cameron Joyce, assistant coach at Northwood University
> in Midland, Michigan, and youngest son of Coach Dru

BEYOND
CHAMPIONSHIPS

BEYOND CHAMPIONSHIPS

A PLAYBOOK
FOR WINNING
AT LIFE

COACH DRU JOYCE II

with Chris Morrow

ZONDERVAN

Beyond Championships
Copyright © 2014 by James Dru Joyce II

This title is also available as a Zondervan ebook. Visit www.zondervan.com/ebooks.

Requests for information should be addressed to:
Zondervan, 3900 *Sparks Dr. SE, Grand Rapids, Michigan 49546*

ISBN 978-0-310-34052-2 (hardcover)

Cover design: Curt Diepenhorst
Cover photography: Dan Davis Photography
Photo insert: All photos courtesy of Coach Dru Joyce II unless otherwise noted
Photo insert background: ©tothzoli001 / Shutterstock
Interior photography: ©moomsabuy / Shutterstock
Interior and photo insert design: Kait Lamphere

First printing January 2015 / Printed in the United States of America

To Carolyn, my wife,
life couldn't have given me a better soul mate and partner.
You have challenged and inspired me to always be better.
You most likely could have done well in life without me,
but I know I could have never made it without you.

With all my love,
Dru.

CONTENTS

FOREWORD
BY LEBRON JAMES

It's hard to believe now, but I was close to the same age my son is today when I first met Coach Dru.

As a young kid in Akron, Ohio, I was like a lot of other kids. I wanted to play basketball and hang out with my friends. So when Coach Dru asked me to play on his team, at the time it was all about basketball. But looking back on it, I now know there was something far greater at work that made me walk into that dusty Salvation Army gym in Akron. Because as much as I wanted to learn and play basketball, what I needed at that point in my life was someone who could show me more than just the X's and O's. Coach Dru taught me about life.

Being raised by a single mom, I knew it was important that I had a male presence in my life — men I could look up to and go to for direction. Prior to meeting Coach Dru, Frank Walker gave me that guidance. When Coach Dru came along, my support system grew, and I related to him on a different level — he knew what it meant to be poor, a feeling I was already too familiar with as a ten-year-old. Most importantly, he knew how to transcend his circumstances, and he wanted to share that knowledge with us too.

That's why I'm so excited for this book. I know firsthand how well these principles work. They worked for me and my brothers — Dru, Sian, Willie, and Romeo — growing up in Akron. My brothers and I were no different from other kids all over the world. We all had dreams. For too many kids, those dreams feel unreachable. But for us, they never did. Because Coach Dru showed us that no matter what sort of obstacles we faced, we could make our dreams a reality.

There are a lot of principles in this book that have become cornerstones of my own philosophy on life. But the principle that has probably impacted me the most is *to always have the heart of a servant.* That's something I learned from Coach Dru, and in many ways it was at the heart of my decision to return to Northeast Ohio as a basketball player.

On the court, the goal will always be to win a title. But off the court, the more important goal remains to shape the lives of young people in the community in the same way that Coach Dru shaped mine. And if I can do that, even just a little bit, then I will have accomplished something that means so much more to me than any championship.

LeBron James,
August 2014

CHAPTER 1

The Beauty of Rock Bottom

> Never confuse a single defeat with a final defeat.
>
> *F. Scott Fitzgerald*

Sensing an upset, the 20,000 fans inside Columbus, Ohio's, Value City Arena are starting to go wild.

Amid the pandemonium, my eyes are focused on Josh Hausfeld, the star player for our opponent, Cincinnati's Roger Bacon High School, as he steps to the line to ice the game. Only seconds remain, and Bacon leads 66 – 63. If Hausfeld makes just one free throw, then the game, our season, and our hope of being named the nation's greatest 2002 high school team will be over.

Compounding the unbelievable frustration my players and I are feeling, Hausfeld is at the line because, moments earlier, my son Li'l Dru had been called for an inexcusable technical foul. A technical that was as much a reaction to the pressure we had all been feeling over the course of that crazy year as it was to the fact that Dru hadn't gotten the ball to attempt a game-tying three-pointer.

Even as I stood there hoping Hausfeld would miss, I had seen this moment coming. Ever since taking over as the head coach of Akron, Ohio's, St. Vincent-St. Mary High School's (STVM) basketball team ten months earlier, I had worried there was no way we could live up to the incredible expectations that had been heaped on us. The expectations that come with being the two-time defending Ohio Division III champs. The expectations that come with being labeled the best high school team in the nation before the season started. The expectations that come when your best player is a lanky seventeen-year-old with a once-in-a-generation talent whose name is LeBron James.

As Hausfeld prepares to put up his first shot, his teammates on the bench gleefully hook their arms together at the crooks of their elbows — the very definition of a connected team. The energy of impending victory is already coursing through the entire lot of them, the glory already held. Behind me, my bench tells a much different story. Each player is on his own island of despair, united only in their common pose — the lower halves of their faces buried in the fronts of their jerseys to conceal the tears. A courtside TV announcer sums up the scene this way: "A lack of composure down the stretch has hurt STVM."

I feel my dismay like a sack of bricks on my chest. Yes, I had seen this moment coming. And no, I hadn't been able to stop it.

Hausfeld takes a deep breath and lets his shot go. It's pure.

With what feels like the eyes of the world on that basketball, we've come up short. A failure that seemed to say so much — about me as a rookie coach, as a father, and as a man.

The day hadn't started off well. Despite being heavy favorites in the game, I had walked into the Value City Arena that day with a thick mess of worry already bubbling up inside of me. I was still getting over a nasty flu and had spent a good part of the previous evening sniffling and shivering. Between tissues and mugs of tea, I had also been forced to corner some of my players in the hotel corridor for having the impudence to party late into the night with the cheerleaders, despite knowing exactly what was at stake the next day. To make matters worse, LeBron woke up that morning with back spasms, and we rushed him to Ohio State for electric pulse treatments, which we hoped would help calm the muscles. But by game time the spasms were back, so I had to make a decision: Do I let him play and hope he can work through the pain, or do I sit him and just have him try to stretch and keep the muscles warm and then see if I can get him in later in the game? I chose to play him.

Despite the ominous signs, my team just *knew* they were going to win. Not because they had prepared better or worked harder than their opponents. But because they were already high from a taste of fame. I had tried to temper their cockiness all season, but the recent *Sports Illustrated* feature that baptized LeBron as "The Chosen One" and the nonstop attention and hoopla that came with all that fuss had helped them tune me out. They were giddy with the confidence that came with so much attention and so many victories already, not to mention the fact that we had already beaten Roger Bacon once that season. Spasms or not for LeBron, the invincibility factor had grown up and around the boys like a stubborn weed, despite this gardener's best efforts.

I didn't walk into the arena that day with such coolness. In fact, it was precisely the pressure of such a game that made me weary of accepting the head coaching job at STVM to begin with. The fact was that I simply didn't want to mess it up. The team already had two state championships under their belts; they now had a chance to win three in a row, which would then put them in a position to win four, something no one has ever done in the state of Ohio. Somehow it felt like I was walking into a catch-22. If we won the state championship, I figured the credit would for sure go to the boys' previous coach, Keith Dambrot. But if we lost, I knew the blame would be mine alone.

And that's exactly how it went.

The Ohio media had a field day with our defeat, putting it squarely in my lap. "Flop at the Top," read one of the headlines;

"Coach Dru Dropped the Ball," quipped another. An article in the *Akron Beacon Journal* split no hairs in its assessment of just what went wrong, claiming that the "main difference between this year's STVM and the past two ... was its leader."

Those words came off the page and seemed to pierce my sense of self the next morning as I stood at our kitchen counter, taking it all in. It's not that I didn't feel responsible; on the contrary, I felt like a captain of a ship that somehow lost course and drove us all into the bluffs. The hard part was knowing that, unlike most first-year high school athletic coaches, who are free to make (and learn from) their mistakes in total anonymity, my shortcomings — given the national notoriety of the team — were in the spotlight for all to see and judge. Not to mention the fact that my son's technical foul essentially sealed the win for Roger Bacon. *My* son.

Li'l Dru was the sole reason I even considered taking on the challenge of coaching boys basketball, and my intentions back then were rooted in the simple desire to be a pillar of support for my son. But the pressures that came with the team's quick ascension into superstardom somehow started to eclipse the simplicity of my original objective, and like the boys I was coaching, I also lost sight of the essence and got caught up with winning and losing.

The night after the game, I lay awake in my bed, replaying each play in my mind's eye, suffering through every unforced turnover and wasted possession, all the while asking myself a series of fundamental questions: Was this whole thing a mistake? Am I in over my head? Am I really cut out for this?

To really appreciate just how confounded I felt, consider that I made the choice to accept this head coaching job in both midlife and midcareer (a career I admittedly wasn't passionate about but one that at least had some stability to it), while being responsible for five mouths to feed.

So when Li'l Dru came into our kitchen the next morning and saw me with my head buried in the palms of my hands and a slew of critical newspaper articles strewn out on the counter, I knew he would understand just how bad I felt. I was consumed with the failure of the moment and wasn't able to see the opportunity for growth that lay in front of me.

Though I may not have seen it at the time, I was forced to call on some key principles that in hindsight not only armed me with the strength to endure the painful aftermath of the defeat but also ultimately helped transform me into a better basketball coach and man.

One of the most important lessons I've learned in life is that the most growth is possible when one stands at rock bottom. And that is exactly where we felt we were after our crushing loss to Roger Bacon. For the team to reclaim our championship — and our integrity — we would have to recommit both collectively and as individuals. Our guys would have to decide to stop playing basketball for themselves, for their parents, for their buddies, for their fans, or even for their future. If they were to climb out of the massive hole they'd dug for themselves, they would have to play only for each other.

CHAPTER 2

Decisions Create
Environment

Man does not simply exist, but always decides what his existence will be, what he will become in the next moment.

Viktor Frankl

Though most of the players on that 2002 high school team were only sixteen or seventeen years old, the journey leading to the championship had actually started several years earlier. The core of that team — LeBron, my son Li'l Dru, and a burly center named Sian Cotton — had been playing together since they were ten and eleven years old, when they first took the floor together at our local Salvation Army's gym on Akron's Maple Street. As I'll relate shortly, after honing their skills during practices at Maple Street, the group began to play in local Amateur Athletic Union (AAU) tournaments. After dominating the local competition, we headed out of Akron (something many of the boys had never done before), cramming into our family's minivan as my wife, Carolyn, and I drove around the Midwest, taking on all comers and even venturing as far as Florida for a national tournament.

Between learning the game and seeing the world (or at least as much of the world as our faithful minivan could carry us to) together, the boys forged a strong bond. Not wanting to go their separate ways once the games and practices were over, LeBron, Sian, and Willie McGee (who joined the team at age thirteen) began sleeping over at our house many nights. I can still hear them down in our basement, watching movies, playing video games, devouring food that Carolyn couldn't seem to make fast enough (*I'm looking at you*, LeBron!), and horsing around in the way young boys everywhere do. Checking in on them late at night, I'd peek into the rec room and see them on the floor wrapped up in their sleeping bags, with empty pizza boxes strewn all around them on the carpet. They might not have been blood, but they were definitely brothers.

They even came up with a nickname for themselves — the Fab Four, an adaptation, of course, from the Fab Five, the nickname of the famous University of Michigan college basketball teams of the early 1990s.

The Fab Four decided to enroll together at St. Vincent-St. Mary as freshmen (a move that was in many ways LeBron's first controversial decision — more on that later). During their sophomore year, they were joined by a young man named Romeo Travis. On paper, Romeo seemed like the perfect candidate to turn the Fab Four into the Fab Five — he had been playing against the guys in various leagues since they were kids and was a very good player himself. But rather than look to break into their group, Romeo had proudly flaunted his independence from it. He didn't have much interest in being the "Fab Fifth." Romeo was more comfortable being a lone wolf than someone who ran with the pack. And rather than trying to help Romeo get past that tendency and invite him into their circle, Li'l Dru, LeBron, Willie, and Sian responded by poking fun at his "me versus the world" attitude and making him feel like even more of an outsider.

As I said, Romeo was an excellent player and his play was critical to the team's success. At six foot seven, he was a tremendous inside presence for us, a fierce rebounder and great leaper who would punctuate lob passes from LeBron with thunderous slam dunks. And he's still throwing them down to this day overseas, where he's played professionally for many years.

Yet back in the winter of 2002, as I looked back at our season and tried to make sense of what had gone wrong, I couldn't help but think that perhaps the uneasy dynamics that existed between the Fab Four and Romeo, their attitudes of invincibility, and all the pressure and expectations placed on the team played a vital part in their loss.

I spent a lot of time that winter and into the spring reflecting on the dynamics and factors that had led to our unraveling. And what I finally decided had done our team in, causing them to come apart at the seams in front of those 20,000 fans, was the simple fact that they had lost their focus.

Don't get me wrong. Had I gathered the guys together in the bowels of the Value City Arena in the moments before the championship game and asked them, "Fellas, are you focused?" they would have answered with a resounding yes. And they probably would even have believed it.

But no matter what they would have *said* to me in the heat of the moment before the big game, their *actions* over the course of the year told a different story. Instead of building an unshakeable foundation on the unique journey they had shared — the practices in hot gyms with no air-conditioning, the endless road trips in our minivan, the countless times they lay on the floor watching VHS tapes late into the night — they chose to become distracted by all the hype of celebrity status.

But the more I thought about it, the more I realized I too had become distracted. I couldn't just coach a basketball team; I had to coordinate and manage the media, entourages of family and friends and hangers-on, ticket requests, and so on — the likes of which hadn't been seen before on a high school stage. I will admit it wasn't an easy task.

I also made the mistake of keeping an assistant coach on staff who eventually tried to undermine what we were trying to accomplish. He had also interviewed for the head coaching job when it became available and was resentful when he didn't get it. His resentment ultimately led to him creating divisions behind my back with some senior players and parents. Instead of helping everyone be on the same page, he encouraged those parents to second-guess my decisions, especially when it came to playing time. All of this came to light early in the season, and I should have asked the coach to step down, which would have been in everyone's best interest. Instead, we tried to work out our differences; but even though we both said the right things, the seeds of mistrust and division had already been planted and taken root.

Our talent covered up most of the internal strife, but the weeds had grown tall by the time of the state championship game, and it cost us. The price was not only the Ohio championship but also a chance at the national championship the kids had been wanting since they were eleven. I can't point a finger at anyone but myself, because the decisions that led to the fracture within the team were my own.

It took that bitter defeat to help me grasp one of the most important lessons I've learned as a coach and as a man: *Decisions create environment.*[*] Whether it's a sixteen-year-old boy struggling with a teammate or a grown man struggling to get his career and life on track, too many people believe they are destined to be a *product* of their environment rather than its *producer.* They have a hard time seeing that their choices are the building blocks of their reality. So every time someone makes a choice, they are essentially mapping out the very scenarios in which their lives will play out.

This is a lesson I want to share in this chapter, using as examples not only the experiences of my team but also some of the ups and downs of my own life. But first let me pose this question: If decisions create environment, what creates decisions? In the best case, it's our

---

[*] A nod to Pastor R. B. Thieme Jr., who used this phrase in a sermon I heard him preach on the biblical principle of sowing and reaping.

intentions. Our intentions are the "why?" in the decisions we make, so the truer and purer our intentions are, the clearer will be the decisions when the time comes to make them. The formula, however, works the other way too. When our intentions are blurry or we are distracted from them, our decision making is inevitably compromised. And sometimes in life we make decisions without really knowing or being connected to our intentions, which may lead to outcomes we don't want or understand.

When we recognize the power of our decisions, whether they are seemingly petty or substantial, every "move" in our life becomes an opportunity to create a new reality, which is an invaluable tool at every age, whether you are a teenager eager to design his destiny as a star athlete or a midlife adult who feels stuck in the rut of an unchangeable monotony.

ROOTS, RAGS, AND RESPONSIBILITY

When I look back at the choices I made at some of the intersections of my own journey, I see several I'm proud of, some less so, and others that became cornerstones of who I am today. The ones that led to the best outcomes were clearly those rooted in my most authentic and positive intentions.

And of all those, the decision that had the most profound impact on the course of my life was my choice to accept Jesus Christ as my Lord and Savior. And like the journeys of many, my journey to Jesus was not a direct one.

I grew up in East Liverpool, a small city in Ohio that sits along the Ohio River, not far from the Pennsylvania and West Virginia borders. In the nineteenth century, East Liverpool was known as "Crockery City," thanks to the more than three hundred potteries that dotted the town, at one time producing over half of the china made in the United States. But by the time I was growing up, calling East Liverpool "Crockery City" was largely an empty boast, with no more than a handful of the town's potteries still in production.

My father toiled arduously as a janitor for a bank and a jewelry store, and my mother as a "day worker," which really meant she was a housekeeper for wealthy white people. Just to make ends meet, sometimes they would both also work as servers at the local country club.

We lived in a small wooden house that sat on a dirt road carved into a steep hill overlooking the Ohio River. The rickety structure had running water and indoor plumbing but not much else. Several of my cousins also lived on the road, and it represented a small pocket of African-American families in the largely white city. A coal furnace heated our home, and I can still remember the truck from the coal company dumping the coal on the hillside on which our home was perched. That hill was so steep that we'd have to erect a barrier so the coal wouldn't roll away. When it rained, the old roof sprang what seemed like dozens of leaks, forcing us to set up buckets all around the house.

Not long ago, like many fathers who fall victim to sentimentality and want to show their sons their roots, I took Li'l Dru (I'll call him Dru or Dru III from now on since he's taller than me) and his younger brother, Cameron, on a trip back to East Liverpool. When we arrived, we found that my Memory Lane was still unpaved, my car's suspension groaning as it made its way over the rocks and potholes that littered my old street. My sons hadn't been back to East Liverpool since they were children, so I knew they could barely connect my past to the way things currently looked. Many of the houses were falling apart and overrun by weeds. In fact, the small trees and weeds had grown so thick along the road that I couldn't even tell where my old home once stood. The road looked vastly different from what I remember as a child. My sons barely looked up from their phones, but I was struck by a sense of poverty I don't remember feeling as a child.

What we might have lacked materially as I was growing up we made up for with community. And one of the places where that sense of togetherness was strongest was at the traditional African Methodist

Episcopal (AME) church we attended. I learned the basic details of the Bible stories and was taught moral principles. But there was little talk of asking Jesus Christ to be our Lord and Savior. While salvation was taught, there was more of an emphasis on joining the church.

One of the most vivid memories I have of that church is the handheld fans given to members of the congregation because of the lack of air-conditioning. During the summer it could get downright scorching, and those fans became my best friends. I still recall that some of them contained illustrations of Bible scenes or other images that had to do with Christianity and prayer. But on one particular fan was the picture of a family — a father, a mother, and their two children, huddled together in a moment of prayer. For some reason, that image stuck with me. There was something about it that resonated deeply with me, though in those days I couldn't put my finger on exactly why.

I was somewhat involved in church as a young person in high school, but you could say I lived life on both ends. I taught Sunday school as a matter of community obligation, but outside of church my life didn't quite jibe with the image of the religious teacher. I wasn't ready to truly accept the role of squeaky-clean church kid, what with my involvement in the usual adolescent shenanigans that most high school kids get into. But it was another incident that pushed me even further away from church.

My pastor had asked me to drive him to a church conference, and before returning home, I went to the restroom. As I was relieving myself, one of the other pastors attending the conference walked in. As he relieved himself, he made a comment to me that was — let's just say it was wildly inappropriate. I didn't say anything in response and never told my pastor about what the man said, but the damage had been done. Like many teenage boys, my antenna was already up for anything I perceived to be hypocrisy on the part of authority figures, and the pastor's comment just cemented my belief that church leaders couldn't be trusted. After that incident, I couldn't get behind whatever else they claimed to stand for. I was generalizing, and I was wrong — but that's how I felt. I thought, *If this is what this is all about, I don't want to be bothered*. I expected more from a pastor, but it seemed they were as sinful as the rest of us.

But all matters of worship and judgment aside, my real identity as a young man during middle school and high school had to do with sports. Everything I did was focused on athletics. It was the essence of who I was, almost as if my *real* church was somewhere out on the football field. From the hillside on which our home sat, you could look down and see exactly half of the town's high school football field near the banks of the river. As a child, my friends and I spent many Friday nights sitting on the hillside and gazing at the illuminated scene below us, patiently waiting for the action to return to the half of field we could see.

When I was old enough to play, I threw myself into the game, even walking two miles to practice every day, since our family didn't have a car until I was in eighth grade.

I was an above-average student, which I attribute to the fact that we only had one school system in our area, and both wealthy and poor kids were enrolled in it. I had already developed a very healthy competitive spirit, and there was no way I was going to sit back and let other kids get better grades than me. I accepted that they had some advantages I didn't enjoy, but school thankfully was a level playing field — one I was determined to show my worth on.

Though it was true that growing up I never viewed my family as poor, when I look back I believe our meager lifestyle and my parents' hard and ceaseless labor planted the first seeds of my intention to prevail as an individual. So after graduating from high school, I did what no one in my family had ever done before: I went to college.

Though getting there was indeed an accomplishment, my university years were fraught with moments that challenged my sense of integrity. I started at Ashland College, which was about two hours west of East Liverpool. Like a lot of kids who go to college for the first time, one of my first impressions as a freshman was that I had some catching up to do socially. Ashland wasn't a big school — it probably didn't have more than two thousand students — but I initially went there to play football. However, when I got to Ashland, I decided not to play, which in hindsight I know wasn't a good decision, because without the discipline of football I began to flounder.

THE TRUTH ABOUT YOUTH

Ashland was a Division III school, and something about it just didn't gel for me. Part of the problem was that like East Liverpool, Ashland was a small town, and the environment began to feel stifling. I had the nagging feeling there were cooler people and bigger parties going on somewhere else. I didn't want to be trapped in a small school in a small town anymore. I longed to go somewhere that offered more fun — a school that had better parties and more people. So I transferred to Ohio University in Athens, Ohio, which at the time seemed like the perfect move.

The summer after my freshman year, I got a job at Crucible Steel in Midland, Pennsylvania, a small town just up the highway from East Liverpool. All of my high school friends who hadn't gone to college were working there. My job was to prep steel samples for chemical analysis, which wasn't bad work. After a couple of weeks, I got used to having money in my pocket and some nice clothes on my back. When the summer began to wind down and it was almost time to go back to school, I decided I would stay at Crucible. Why spend money to go to college and be broke in the hope that my education would someday help me make a better living when I was already making a decent living at Crucible?

Thankfully my mother, who clearly held a bigger vision for me, put her foot down and insisted that college come first. "You're going to finish this," she said with a no-nonsense finality, and despite my begrudging, her words became my personal mantra after I returned to school. Four years later, the steel mill closed down, leaving lots of those guys jobless and hanging out on the corner of East Liverpool with absolutely nothing to do. *Decisions create environment* — and since I wasn't yet mature enough to own that truth, I was fortunate my mother's decision kept me focused and on track.

Ohio University had more than 18,000 students, and at first the larger campus seemed to give me some of the energy and excitement I was craving. But it was also a Division I school, which meant any hopes I harbored for my football career were effectively dashed. Initially I was fine with that. Without football dominating my schedule, I had more time to hang out, get high, and chase girls.

I had gained the social scene I was looking for, but I soon realized I'd begun to lose my sense of self. Despite complaining about how much of my time it took up, football had been a very important part of my life. It had given me a sense of purpose and taught me valuable lessons about how to structure my life and be disciplined. Without it, I began to drift.

Because I didn't have football to ground me, and because I'd fallen in with a group of guys who didn't value school at Ohio U, I did what most kids do when they're not sure *how* to be or *who* to be: I simply tried to fit in. On most days we'd strut around campus, do the bare minimum to get by in our classes, and spend the rest of the afternoons getting high, playing ball, flirting with girls, or just hanging out. There was no real sense of purpose, no commitment to anything other than ourselves, which back then, was just fine by us.

The days when I was determined to prove my worth through academics had become a foggy memory. Instead, the "respect" of my peers became my motivation. For better or worse, in black America (and probably beyond), too many young men feel they must earn their reputations by holding their own and acting tough. At Ohio University I found myself among guys from cities like Cleveland, Cincinnati, Akron, and Detroit who had a swagger and toughness I hadn't learned back in East Liverpool. There was no way I wasn't going to hold my own among them. I even used to lie to people about where I was from, fearing they would respect me less if they knew I came from such a small town. Without a sense of who I was, I felt I had no choice but to be like them.

So while I thought I was making decisions that would help me to fit in, they were ultimately choices that led me into a downward spiral by forcing me to project an image that really wasn't me. There is no constraint on what an ego will do when a person lacks a moral compass, and back then, I didn't have any kind of compass except for the one that told me to *belong*.

After one year at Ohio University, I was so burnt-out from all the partying and drugs that I decided to take a semester off and clean up a bit with the help of my sister, JoAnne. She was eighteen years older than me and lived in New York City, and I had spent every summer with her growing up. Her husband had been ill and passed away that year, so she was glad to have me around. I ended up staying with her for several months, and to some degree, I did manage to clean up my act. Yes, I was still smoking weed, but the extreme partying was definitely starting to taper off — or so it seemed.

Unfortunately, whatever progress I managed to make in New York quickly dissipated when I returned to school in January. Within a matter of days, I slipped back into my old pattern of poor decision making, for no other reason than it was what my friends were doing. And for the next year and a half, I pretty much stayed in that rut — slacking hard and getting caught up in a life that had absolutely nothing to do with who I really was.

Looking back on it, probably the thing I regret the most during that period was dating multiple women simultaneously. Because it's one thing to not be true to yourself; it's another thing altogether to lie to someone else about your intentions. And I was telling these young women whatever I thought would make me seem hip or cool, without any regard for consequence or, more importantly, for *their feelings*. I kept behaving that way until a situation really shook me as

I entered my senior year. My pastor likes to refer to this type of thing as a "significant emotional event," which is essentially a life-changing moment that forces a person to look in the mirror and ask himself the hard, important questions.

BECOMING WHO YOU ARE

On an exceptionally crisp autumn morning in September, I found myself staring at my reflection in the fogged-up mirror of a small trailer I had been renting. And the harder I stared, the less I liked what I saw. Had I been able to grasp back then the fact that decisions create environment, I might have thought twice about how I had played my cards.

My inability to make the right choices concerning these women caused a lot of unnecessary pain. I felt somehow justified in my actions because I believed it was something all the boys were doing, so it seemed OK. However, as I began to have feelings for each of the women, it became increasingly harder for me to continue being involved with all of them. But I selfishly refused to let any of them go, and none of them were willing to let me go, even though they knew I had other women in my life. I liked being wanted by them. But it all came crashing down when the summer before my senior year, one of them told me she was pregnant. The news alone would have been enough to jolt me, but add to this the fact that I had made a choice to marry one of them — Carolyn.

Carolyn had certainly pushed me to want to make some changes in my life, to be a better person, so this unanticipated pregnancy with another woman felt like twenty giant leaps backward after I'd inched a few baby steps forward. My feelings for Carolyn notwithstanding, I knew I had to do the right thing, which was to take responsibility for my actions, marry the other girl, and help take care of our baby. I now had to share this with Carolyn, which is another example of the environments that our decisions create.

I returned to OU in the fall with my pregnant girlfriend. We had decided to get married in Athens. As I was preparing for the arrival of our child, she shocked me with yet more unexpected news: she wasn't pregnant. I experienced a huge wave of relief when I learned she wouldn't be having our baby. And after that wave passed, I knew I had to follow my heart. The revelation that she wasn't carrying our child severed whatever was left of my feelings for her, and even though she still cared about me, I recklessly pushed her out of my life. My wrong decision to date multiple women put me in a situation, an environment, that caused a lot of pain.

In that moment in the little trailer when I was washing my face and looking in the mirror, I felt God was showing me who I had become. I saw a man who behaved without regard for consequences, a man so wrapped up in ego that he had lost sight of almost every-thing else, a man who lived only for himself. And I knew I had to change. Almost intuitively, I came right out and asked Jesus to save me because I didn't want to be this person anymore. *Lord*, I pleaded, *please come into my life and help me be the person You want me to be.* That was my prayer, and it was also the moment that ignited my spiritual journey. This decision to ask for God's help and to remain receptive to it set the tone for what the rest of my life would look like. That doesn't mean I had an overnight transformation, but my life definitely began to change.

Now I had to make things right with Carolyn. I knew I owed her a proper explanation. But by this time she had moved on. There was someone else in her life. I made up my mind that day — again, a landmark *decision* — that if there was even a shred of hope, I had to pursue it. I was not going to give up until I felt there was no hope left. Carolyn had not returned to OU, so during my Thanksgiving break, I went to see her at her parents' home in Pittsburgh. Not only did I have to win her back, but I had to face her parents as well, who I was quite sure wouldn't be too happy to see me either. They knew I had hurt her.

I approached the front door of her parents' home, my heart

pounding and hands shaking. Her father came to the door with a look in his eyes that said, *How dare you?* To his credit, he managed to invite me in, and we engaged in some awkward small talk. Then Carolyn walked in, and right away I could tell she wasn't happy to see me. She eyed me cautiously as I explained everything to her: the false pregnancy and the breakup. I also allowed her to see me standing in front of the mirror, ashamed to see the guy who was looking back at me. To see how I had cried out to God for help and felt convicted that one of the first steps toward making things right was to try to be the man she deserved.

She let me know she wasn't too pleased by what she heard, and I couldn't blame her. No matter how much I felt I had changed, the reality was that I had messed up terribly. Yet, even though I knew she was unhappy with me, when I left her house that evening, I had hope. I knew I wasn't saying good-bye forever. I still had a chance.

At the end of Thanksgiving break, I returned to campus, where I spent several days just wandering around consumed with the sense that I needed to search for a better way to live. A better relationship with the world. I had one friend who was very spiritual, but not in a traditionally religious way, and he and I would get into profound philosophical discussions late into the night. He gave me books to read about Buddhism and Hinduism — all kinds of literature from different places around the world. I enjoyed reading those books and gaining an understanding of how other people understood the concept of faith. But I also couldn't help feeling like I was searching for something that was right there in front of me, and that something was Jesus. And I was looking for Him everywhere *but* in the church. Despite the disillusionment I had experienced with the church, I was still predisposed to Christianity. I had grown up in it and still felt its teachings calling me — even if at times softly — back home. So despite all those nights searching through various esoteric texts, I found that my quest for meaning was a roundabout journey back to the Bible. I enjoyed my trip, but ultimately my earnest desire was to reconnect with Christ.

When I settled the question of who I would follow, I began to get a clearer understanding of sin and forgiveness. I stopped expecting so much from others and being so critical, and I wasn't as quick to throw stones as I had been before. I yearned to become less reckless with people and their lives. Until then, I had behaved selfishly and irresponsibly toward others, and my "significant emotional event" showed me just how wrong that really was. Returning to the faith I had been taught, I became more in tune with the concept of "missing the mark," which is exactly what sin is — and something we're all prone to. Missing the mark doesn't make a person more evil or less valuable than someone else, because spiritual work is an ongoing journey we all have to take. A lot of people tend to look for answers when negative things happen to them, but in my case it was *my own* negative actions that sparked my quest for more meaning. I began to understand how spirituality and the awareness of a higher source of truth reshape not only your sense of self but your overall environment as well.

In the meantime, I had been writing a steady stream of letters to Carolyn, keeping her updated on what was happening in my life and reminding her of how much I wanted her to be part of it. (Let me add that while technology has changed the world for the better in many ways, it saddens me that people no longer write letters to each other. If you're as old as I am, then I'm sure you remember how much effort went into writing one of those long letters — but also how much they ultimately affected the person who received the letter.)

In one of my epic correspondences, I summed up the courage I hadn't been able to muster in person and proposed to Carolyn. Which she, in turn, declined at first. But perhaps because her "no" was delivered by the United States Postal Service instead of in person, I didn't give up.

Instead, when I finished school, I moved back to East Liverpool, which was only an hour from Pittsburgh, to be close to her and started hunting for a job. And I'm still pleased to say that once I arrived back home, she began to soften her stance and agreed to marry me, but on one condition — that we wait to tie the knot until she finished school.

Although it was a perfectly reasonable request — not only were we still very young, but I was also not too far removed from having treated her very badly — I wouldn't settle for that compromise. I was almost overcome with a craving for real change and was incredibly focused on redesigning my life in a positive way. And despite my young age and relative lack of maturity, I still somehow knew marriage to Carolyn was the change I was seeking. I was beyond ready — so ready that I gave Carolyn an ultimatum: "If you won't marry me, I'm not going to stay around." I let it be known that my older sister had a job lined up for me in New York, and I was prepared to take it if Carolyn couldn't commit to our future together in Pittsburgh (a total bluff, as leaving her was the last thing I wanted to do).

This time, Carolyn's mom saved the day. The same woman who just months earlier had been skeptical of me and my intentions stepped in and proved once again that "mother knows best" when she gave her daughter the words of wisdom that helped Carolyn make a crucial decision of her own. "When a man is ready to get married, if he doesn't marry you, then he's going to marry someone else," said Carolyn's mother — and I guess that did it, because shortly thereafter, we became husband and wife.

During our first few years, we were still getting to know each other, but we were committed to the principle of marriage, aware we'd face some ups and downs. For starters, I had just begun my job, and we were living in one small room in her parents' home while we saved up money. Also, I was early in my spiritual quest, and I could tell that Carolyn couldn't relate to a lot of the literature I was interested in exploring. Carolyn was raised in the church, and unlike me, who felt the need to occasionally wander outside of it, Carolyn has never wavered, right up to this very day.

But as challenging as it all was, as a couple we made the decision to never run from it, to never take the easy way out, and, no matter what, to always see things through. That joint decision paved the way for thirty-six years of marriage and the birth of our four wonderful children — showing both of us again just how much power one decision can truly hold.

All these years later, I still remember how as Carolyn walked down the aisle, looking so beautiful on our wedding day, I had a flashback to an image from my childhood — the picture I had seen on the handheld fan at my parents' church. I understood in that moment the reason the picture of the family on the fan had resonated so deeply with me. Somewhere deep inside, I knew it was exactly what I wanted for myself. As a boy, holding that fan and gazing at that image, I guess I intuitively knew it was the environment I wanted to see myself in someday. And as my lovely bride came toward me, I realized I was on the path to obtain that and more. I realized, after all the years of running around and partying, chasing women, and having no real sense of purpose, our marriage would not only show me just how lost I had been but also provide a proving ground where I would become determined to be the best version of myself. That is the moment when I felt my life really begin to be put in order. The big lesson here is that until we're willing to admit the part we've played, we won't be able to fix whatever has been broken.

After a year of living with Carolyn's parents, we moved into our first apartment, and our life together began to take shape. It was in that apartment that Carolyn became pregnant with our first two children.

These were some of the greatest times of my life, as my vision of having a family had come to life in the most glorious way. I was a husband and a father, and after I graduated from Ohio University in 1978, I landed a job in sales at ConAgra, the company behind brands like Hunt's tomato products, Wesson cooking oil, and Peter Pan peanut butter, to name a few. I had initially gone to a headhunter's office, where I naively declared I wanted to go into banking, not knowing the first thing about what that even required. I somehow managed to make my degree seem like some version of a business degree, and one of the executives suggested I try my luck at sales. Without a better option, I interviewed for the job at ConAgra and got it. It came with a car, which they promised to update every three years. I didn't know a thing about sales — nor did I care to, really. To be honest, at the time I thought the car was the real perk in landing this position, not to mention the medical benefits and sense of security that came with receiving a paycheck every two weeks.

During those five years in Pittsburgh, the job allowed me to be close enough to my hometown to keep in touch with some of my old friends. I started playing flag football, which helped me reconnect with a piece of my identity that had somehow checked out during college. I was finally coming back to myself and evolving into the man I was always meant to be, secure with the realization that my decision to stay in college not only made me the first in my family to graduate but also led me to meet and marry the true love of my life.

NO RISK, NO REWARD

Despite the steadiness of my job and all its perks, as well as the peace of mind it provided my wife and me as we raised our kids, I left a stable source of income to pursue my dream of becoming a full-time coach. Next to surrendering my life to Jesus and marrying Carolyn, it was the most important decision of my life.

Several years earlier when I had started to coach part-time, a part of me knew I had found my purpose. I had found something that brought me joy — working with kids and helping bring them into adulthood. I became alive in the gym, in the faces of these kids whose lives would hopefully be affected positively through my guidance. Nothing felt more important.

But despite these positive feelings that were brewing, I couldn't help feeling bad about my performance at work. My sales numbers looked good, but I knew they could have been better. I knew my real day began at the end of my workday. And as I grew as a coach and the success of my team increased, it became more and more difficult to reconcile my desire to coach with holding down a job in corporate America.

Perhaps because of my gradually dwindling desire to be at ConAgra, during my last year there, I was given a less than favorable performance review and was placed on probation. I don't hold a grudge against the company, but it was looking to downsize and needed to build a case against me to warrant such a move. I met with my bosses, who gave me a choice either to move to a failing account in Syracuse, New York (only because I had twenty-five years with the company), or to take a severance package and call it a day. In that moment, I gave them an answer with my mouth — "Yes, I'll take the position at the Syracuse account" — but the whole time my heart was saying no.

My first instinct, with my wife and kids front and center in my mind, was to stick with the company. After all, we had just built our house and bought a new car for my wife. Our daughters had graduated from college; Dru was finishing his first year at the University of Akron; and Cameron was a freshman in high school. So it wasn't like we didn't need an income.

My original goal was to just coast through a few more years. But it didn't happen that way. You can't resist what is. You have to move in what is. It's about staying in the present moment and flowing with the reality that exists right under your nose. It's also about knowing that we honor God when we honor our authentic self, and that following the paths to our dreams is one such way to do this. If we work at it and do it in a way that glorifies God, He'll honor our effort. If you are actively involved in this life, you can do great things.

On that day I gave my employers what I believed was my final answer, I got into the car and headed home. On the way, I called my wife and told her what had happened and how torn I felt, and both of us cried, knowing we were on the threshold of real change. Later that evening, we talked and made a decision to leave ConAgra and trust God to provide for our needs. We had always said we believed God to be a provider, but that day we decided to put that belief to the test. So with my wife's blessing and a mountain of faith, I went into the human resources office the next morning and told them I had changed my mind.

"You don't want to go down this path," the HR exec said, looking at me ominously, "because if you do, there's no turning back."

But by then I was sure. "Let's do this," I said. "I'm done."

Fortunately, the company's severance package would get me from May to the next January, for which I was thankful, because, truth be told, they weren't obligated to give me anything. If I had stayed, right now I'd be at thirty-five-plus years, and I could have retired with a full pension.

As scary as it was to walk away from a job security that many would covet, I found strength in the realization that I was a lot more creative and resourceful than I had given myself credit for. I wanted to build a business around basketball, so in my first year out of corporate America, I put together fifty AAU teams, and with our savings I somehow made enough money to sustain us *and* thrive, because for the first time, I was doing something that was close to my heart.

Eventually in 2006, I began organizing the King James Shooting Stars Classic travel team basketball tournament, earning twice as much as I ever made in corporate America. If I had stayed in the comfort zone of what I like to call "stuck stability," I would've never been able to recognize any of this.

While it is crucial to have a livelihood, I think it's equally imperative to stay focused on what you want to get done. You must steel yourself against having the typical anxieties that can come with taking chances, fight the doubt that tries to creep in, and have faith that things are going to be all right. You may have to sacrifice the certainty that comes with a biweekly paycheck, but in my case, it has been ten years since I walked away from corporate America, and I'm proud to say I haven't missed a meal or a house payment — and, most important of all, I haven't looked back.

And once you hear what the whispers of your heart are saying, you need to act. This type of action usually comes with a certain degree of risk. In my case, the risk came in the form of the prospect of getting irregular paychecks, losing my corporate benefits, and giving up any possibility of ever climbing the ranks at ConAgra.

And that was only one end of it. On the other side was the risk I would fail as an entrepreneur and wouldn't bring in enough money to support my family. If I would have allowed the anxiety to consume me, I would have failed for sure. I had to make a concerted effort to chisel away at that built-in stress and keep my eye on the goal, undeterred and resolute. Had I caved to the anxiety, I'd probably still be working in sales today, looking blankly at a spreadsheet.

So I began to mobilize. I tell my kids that once you make a decision, you can't look back. I learned this lesson when one of my ConAgra colleagues questioned my choices. "Where are you going? Where's your new job?" he asked. He also proceeded to say, "You don't ever leave a job without a new one lined up." I knew this type of dialogue wasn't going to help me. If I kept talking to him, it would have shaken my faith.

Ironically, as a coach I once almost said to a player, "Don't turn down a scholarship without having another one lined up" — but then I caught myself. He was about to embark on his own faith walk, so I knew I had to let it go. He eventually got a scholarship, but it only came after a year as a walk-on player. Sometimes things don't happen as quickly as we would like, but we have to be willing to stay the course.

When I finally left ConAgra, I went as far as to not contact people I used to work with, people I considered to be real friends too.

I went as far as to not call them back because I couldn't afford to hear about office politics and gossip. At that point, everything felt fragile and uncertain, but I intuitively knew I couldn't stop midstream and look back. As Scripture poignantly teaches, "No one who puts a hand to the plow and looks back is fit for service in the kingdom of God" (Luke 9:62).

Over the years, after settling into this new chapter of my life, I have been able to reconnect with some of those people and explain my behavior. Whatever dissatisfaction I felt with my job, they had been good coworkers and friends, and they deserved an explanation — especially since, with the success of our teams, they might have thought my lack of communication stemmed from me getting "big time" on them. Which couldn't have been further from the truth. "I couldn't afford to doubt my path," I told several of my coworkers when we reconnected. "I felt that continuing our relationship wouldn't have been the best thing moving forward." Because I was sincere, I don't believe anyone took it personally. In fact, the real friends among them understood and applauded my will to follow my dreams.

And thank God I did follow my dreams because in 2008 – 2009, I led St. Vincent-St. Mary to its fifth state championship. And even though our championship loss in 2002 stung badly, I'm proud of what I've accomplished as a head coach at STVM. During my 13 seasons, my record is 251 wins and 87 losses, and our teams have won 11 district championships, 7 regional championships, and 3 state championships.

Working with young people for all these years, I'm always struck by how when we're young we tend to get so caught up in the short term — *How will this affect me now? How will this impact my life today?* — that we don't take the long term into consideration, forcing us to lose sight of the big picture. That's why I like to remind kids that, while things can *seem* to work out in the short term, their plan has to extend beyond today or tomorrow. They have to ask, *Where am I going to be three [or five or ten] years from now, and how am I going to get there?*

I am a firm believer in living in the present moment, but while we do so, we must remember to make decisions that will serve to enhance our entire future.

Every time you make a decision, you are making a personal judgment about your current self, your vision for yourself, and your values. You need to recognize that every decision won't please everyone, but if it's the best one for you, then you need to run with it and not allow "the voices" to take you off the path. If I can distill anything from those early days, it is the idea that we all have the power to shape not only our own futures but also our current realities, no matter what the perceived challenges. Understanding our intentions leads us on a path of responsible choice — and our choices shape an environment that will give us more options in life.

As my pastor, Bishop Johnson, says, "You have choice. And your choice has impact on your direction. And if you don't use your choice, don't blame God; don't blame the people around you; and don't blame your circumstances. You can always exercise your choice."

THE DECISION

Now I don't think I could get away with wrapping up this chapter without mentioning two of the most famous decisions in the basketball world — decisions I certainly followed very closely. Yes, I'm talking about "The Decision" in which LeBron went on ESPN to announce which team he would be signing with as a free agent in the summer of 2010, as well as the decision he made in 2014 to return to Cleveland.

I don't think I need to rehash the reaction to The Decision (it's so famous that it even has its own Wikipedia page), but suffice it to say that everyone involved would probably agree it could have been handled differently. I remember saying to someone at the time, "It's fine to break up with your girlfriend if you're in a bad relationship; just don't do it on national TV."

And while I've never spoken to LeBron specifically about The Decision, I think he'd agree with that assessment. Even though he clearly never meant any harm by it, The Decision left a bad taste in people's mouths for several years.

But I do want to point to a few things about The Decision that got overlooked in the media and public frenzy that ensued. More than anything, The Decision put Bron (a nickname I often use with LeBron) in a better place to work out his destiny. As I see it, that's what's important. He made a choice that allowed him to strategize his life plan. No matter what anyone says, he created an environment for himself that led him to four straight NBA Finals. We know that his decision also created some anger from those outside. Some people even burned his jersey in protest — but at the end of the day, that's their choice. That's life. Decisions are going to be criticized and subjected to scrutiny.

The Decision also created an environment for the Boys & Girls Clubs of America, the nonprofit group that received a donation from Bron of almost 2.5 million dollars, which came directly from the 6 million dollars in charity revenue from the ESPN show. For a nonprofit group that had seen its budget slashed over the years, this was an incredibly impactful donation. That aspect of The Decision was quickly overshadowed, but I believe it should have been celebrated and gotten more focus than anything else.

On a personal level, it's worked out great for Bron. Though many folks had speculated that he chose Miami so he could indulge in the South Beach lifestyle, since he joined the Heat in 2010, he married his lovely wife, Savannah, and became settled into and dedicated to family life. So on both a basketball and a personal level, we have to say The Decision was the right one.

As I write this, Bron has made a new decision to return to Cleveland, which I see as correct too. He has grown and matured and now realizes that his heart is still in Northeast Ohio. The reaction to his return has been far different from when he left. Fans have welcomed him back with open arms. His relationship with Cleveland Cavaliers owner Dan Gilbert has been restored, and the region is electrified. Bron may have changed residences, but no matter how far he went, he really never moved, because home is where the heart is.

Both of these decisions should serve as an inspiration for anyone trying to make a tough choice in life. While your decisions can be criticized and subjected to scrutiny (though doubtfully on the scale of Bron's), if they reflect what's in your heart and point you toward where you want to go in life, eventually the storm of scrutiny will pass — and when it does, you'll find yourself in a much happier place.

Bron's last decision also gives credence to the fact that sometimes things have to come full circle before there can be completion. His career began in Cleveland, and it will end in Cleveland. Just like competitive basketball as a youth started for him on Maple Street at a Salvation Army gym, and his high school career ended at St. Vincent-St. Mary on Maple Street.

CHAPTER 3

The Myth of the Self-Made Man

There is no such thing as a self-made man. We are made up of thousands of others. Everyone who has ever done a kind deed for us or spoken a word of encouragement to us has entered into the make-up of our character and of our thoughts as well as our success. *George Matthew Adams*

want you all to think back to last November. The fifteenth to be exact. What did you have for dinner that night?"

Like most of the folks sitting inside The House of the Lord congregation that summer Sunday morning, I was unsure not only of what I'd eaten for dinner those many months before but also of exactly what my pastor, Bishop Joey Johnson, was trying to get at.

I had come a long way in my attitude toward the clergy since I was a teenager. As I'll relate shortly, I had come to view Bishop Johnson as one of the most positive influences in my life, a man who, time and time again, had managed to plant little seeds of wisdom deep into my consciousness.

So rather than join in the confused murmur that was spreading through the pews, I wanted Bishop Johnson to reveal the piece of truth he was undoubtedly hiding up his sleeve. And after a perfectly timed beat, he did.

"You may not remember what you ate for dinner that night — and I don't remember what I ate either," he said. "But one thing is for sure, and it applies to each and every one of us sitting in this room and beyond. That meal, as far away and forgotten as it may now seem, managed to nourish us with its nutrients. That meal helped the younger ones among us grow, just as it helped sustain the older ones among us." Some members of the congregation closed their eyes, trying to internalize the pastor's message; my eyes were fixed on him, eager to understand.

"Ladies and gentlemen, I'm here to tell you that this very specific meal we cannot even remember in the midst of so many others we have been blessed with since, nevertheless helped — even in the tiniest, most miniscule way — to make us who we are at this very moment. Believe it or not, that meal had an impact."

Bishop Johnson had settled into an easy yet gripping cadence, and the congregation was with him every step of the way. "It was part of the *everything* that shapes us" he said. "Part of the flow of life's many pieces that lends to our evolution. And let me tell you — the people in our lives do the very same thing."

Bishop Johnson acknowledged a few amens and continued. "The mentors in our lives, however big or small their impact on us may be, are there to nourish us as humans, so that we can grow as individuals and truly become the most vital, strongest versions of ourselves imaginable."

As I said, Bishop Johnson dropped a lot of jewels on me over the years, and I expect he'll drop several more. The concept I took with me out of church that Sunday morning is one I will hold on to for the rest of my life — the awareness that so many of the people in my life, whether or not they knew it — were elemental in my growth as a man.

I needed every last drop of their mentoring. As a young man, I prided myself on rejecting certain forms of authority and trying to blaze my own path, yet now, in retrospect, I can see I was only able to stay on that path with the help of the shepherding presence of many different people.

Which is why I feel that one mistake we make as Americans, and especially as men, is exalting what I call "the myth of the self-made man."

Yes, hard work and determination, especially in those who have overcome hardships and discrimination, are traits that should be lauded. But no matter how hard we work at pulling ourselves up by the bootstraps, those straps are made of leather, not steel. They can, and often do, break.

As someone who works every day with young people who seem determined to prove they can indeed do it alone, I've learned that the right mentorship can often be the difference between success and failure, not just in sports but in all aspects of life. This ability to remain a presence in a young person's life, even when they feel they don't need it and think it's holding them back, is what makes being a coach such a sacred position. This role is something to be thankful for and one that must be honored and respected. It is a remarkable opportunity to truly make a difference.

More than winning any championship, knowing I get to be a stable presence in a young person's life precisely when they need it the most is an incredible blessing.

OUR TEACHERS ARE EVERYWHERE

I was fortunate. My first mentors lived right under my roof — my parents. Their hard work, focus on faith, and belief in education took root in my mind at a very young age. I would have to carve out my own path through the temptations of youth to truly see just how invaluable their principles and self-sacrifice were, but they instilled in me a set of values that set the tone for who I would eventually become and what I would believe in. I meet a lot of kids from single-parent homes or from homes with parents who are virtually absent, who struggle mightily to carve out that path. It makes me hold close to my heart the lessons of fortitude and togetherness I got from my own home.

Mine was an extended family. We had the kind of household where the kids spent a lot of time with cousins, aunts, and uncles. My older sister, JoAnne, who, as I said earlier, is eighteen years older than me, never felt at home in East Liverpool. Early on, she went to New York to live with one of our aunts. Being so much younger, I never dreamed of trying to do such a thing myself, but the fact that JoAnne had the courage to up and go always impressed me. She was smart and fearless, and I was in complete awe of her.

My sister was determined to make a life for herself in New York, and she wasted no time making sure it happened. She got married at the age of twenty, and so began her path as a woman who knew what she wanted. She was one of the first to show me that change is possible, as long as you're willing to take hold of the reins and make that change.

From the time I was in first grade all the way to high school, the day after the school year ended, I'd be sitting on a plane to spend every summer in Saint Albans, Queens, where my sister lived. There were many kids in that neighborhood, and we all quickly became friends. From the moment I hit town, I would immediately fall into their rhythm of playing stickball, chasing ice cream trucks through the streets, hanging out on stoops, and laughing our way through the sizzle of July. New York was a magical flurry of education, stimulation, culture, and friendships that lasted well into my adulthood. Having grown up in a small town on a tiny little street, where most of my friends were my relatives, life in the big city represented diversity and possibility.

Later in life, I came across Malcolm Gladwell's famous book *Outliers*, in which he talks about the Baltimore school district's attempt to understand why certain ethnic groups struggled. The researchers noticed that when they tested the kids at the beginning of the school year, everyone was testing about the same, and during the middle of the school year, the testing didn't vary a whole lot either. The big jump came over the summer, because most of the African-American kids were inner-city kids who didn't have the opportunity to experience much of anything over the break, while kids from more privileged parts of society got to do things like travel and go to camp — experiences that seemed to accelerate their learning.

Well, that's exactly what I gained during those summers in St. Albans with my sister. While being in New York City will expose people to many interesting experiences, St. Albans in particular was home to so much culture. Count Basie, John Coltrane, James Brown, Miles Davis, Ella Fitzgerald, Lena Horne, Joe Lewis, Jackie Robinson, Roy Campanella, W. E. B. Du Bois, and Roy Wilkins had all called this neighborhood home before I arrived. And future stars like Al Roker and LL Cool J were growing up there around the same time I was there. Walking the streets, you could almost feel the history around you. Knowing I was walking the same streets that Miles Davis or Jackie Robinson had walked inspired me and pushed me to try to reach the same heights they had. My sister, a true mentor, sensed the impact St. Albans was having on me and made sure to expose me to as much as possible. By the end of each summer, I'd go back to East Liverpool loaded with information and genuinely inspired by the world.

You know the saying, "small town, small mind" — to me it represents the idea of people who aren't willing to budge outside of their comfort zones, those who are stubbornly unwilling to expand beyond what they know or where they know. I had a few friends growing up who were stuck with that small-town mind-set, and seeing my sister venture out beyond East Liverpool, especially in a place as magical as St. Albans, was downright revolutionary. Although I appreciated the closeness and comfort of East Liverpool, it was incredibly helpful to know that a larger world not only was out there but was accessible.

Which is why I encourage my players to see as much of the world as possible. If they have an aunt in New York or a cousin in Los Angeles they can visit during the summer, I want them to get a taste of that lifestyle if possible. And if I was coaching kids in New York City, I would encourage them to visit relatives who lived in the country during the summer. No matter where you live, it's easy to get caught up in not only the rhythms but also the gossip and dramas of your immediate surroundings. That's one of the main reasons I was willing to go on those long drives to Memphis or Florida with Dru III, LeBron, and the rest of the Shooting Stars (more about them shortly) when they were kids. Sure, staying at a hotel in a strip mall outside of Memphis might not have been the same as visiting St. Albans in the 1960s, but for those kids it was big. LeBron had never been outside of Akron, so I know to see there was a world outside of it — one he could compete in and win in — was a big motivator for him and the other kids too.

Even though I learned so much during those summers in St. Albans, mentors can appear in small towns too. A great example is one of my high school football coaches, Larry Fernandez. In a small, rural town like East Liverpool, where the main industries were pottery, dishware, and steel and where most folks had blue-collar jobs, there were few solid African-American role models — especially those you might describe as intellectuals or professionals. Coach Fernandez was a young African-American guy who had just graduated from college, and he did bring those qualities into our lives. He coached football and track *and* he was a teacher, and I liked everything about the lifestyle he led. He didn't just talk to us about sports; he spoke to us about life. And whether or not I (or he) knew it at the time, he definitely planted the coaching bug in me.

He leveled with us. He told us he knew what it was like to be young and want to have fun, but he also knew that if you're not prepared for life, it will chew you up and spit you out. To drive the message home, he used examples of people we knew and could see around us in East Liverpool. Individuals who were still joking around and treating life like a party, even though now the joke was on them. Guys who were good athletes ten or fifteen years ago but were now just hustlin' or hangin' around the bars of East Liverpool and clearly didn't have a plan to do anything other than that. Larry said that no matter how great an athlete you were in high school, you have to have a big-picture plan that transcends the here and now, because where high school stops, life begins — and if you don't have a plan, you don't have much of anything.

Coach Fernandez was one of the voices, along with those of my parents, who encouraged me to go to college. It was a monumental decision because my parents never conceived of going to college; they didn't even graduate from high school. And most of the folks from their generation in East Liverpool had similar backgrounds.

In fact, Larry was the only African-American college-educated person I knew at that time. Other older kids graduated before I did and went off to college, but none of the ones I knew came back with a degree. Larry moved forward to be a coach and an educator, and ultimately he went on to become the principal of a school in his hometown of Weirton, West Virginia.

Coach Fernandez was an effective mentor because his life served as a blueprint I could follow. He was a living testament to the idea that sometimes more is caught than taught because he showed me by example how to live a life of integrity and self-worth. The way he carried himself made an impact on me, and I wanted to emulate that for the guys I coach, have coached, and will continue to coach.

It was one thing to have a mentor who came with football, which was something I loved and felt an affinity for, but there would also be mentors around even when I was immersed in situations that weren't nearly as favorable to me.

Case in point: Jim Rocco, an older Italian gentleman who mentored me during my first job out of college at ConAgra. As I said earlier, good mentorship is often the difference between failure and success, and whether or not I cared about sales, after a few years I was promoted to the position of senior sales rep, and later key account manager, which for my family and me was a big deal. Even though I knew in a fundamental way that corporate America was not really my thing, Jim single-handedly taught me everything I know about being a good businessman and armed me with invaluable skills that would serve me well in many of the entrepreneurial challenges I would take on in life. I can honestly say I love him to this day.

My family also benefited from the positive mentorship of my pastor, whose powerful insights I shared as this chapter began. Bishop Johnson would say to us, "God is a God of excellence, so that's just what we have to give back to Him — excellence." His own life illustrated that pursuit, having started his church with only four people in his mother's living room — a church he managed to build into a two-thousand-member congregation called The House of the Lord.

He has had a tremendous impact on my wife and me, on the way we raised our children, and on how we lead our lives. Carolyn and I have been married for thirty-six years, but when we first came to the church, we were in the fifth year of our marriage, and it was through the support and counsel of Bishop Johnson that we were able to sustain our relationship through some of our most challenging times. He helped us understand how to relate to one another and even how to parent our kids. In today's world, there are classes and courses for just about everything, but for the most important job you will likely ever have — being a parent — there is no such class. However, our pastor gave us the building blocks to lay the right kind of foundation.

Thanks not only to his legacy of wisdom and support, but also to the congregation he built over the years, I was fortunate to meet other like-minded individuals who helped me on my path and who also, each in their own way, became pivotal figures in my professional, personal, and spiritual journey. The lesson is that a great by-product of mentorship is the chance to network and build community because ultimately the right people lead you to the right people.

SHOW, DON'T TELL

I decided the way to be a good coach is to be a good person. I knew I would be judged as a coach by our opponents, by the public, by the parents, and by wins and losses. But I also understood I'd be judged by God on how I influenced the young lives He had entrusted to me.

A gentleman at the church ran a program called Say Yes to Tennis, which taught inner-city kids how to play the sport. My two daughters, along with Dru, had been involved in it, which gave me a glimpse into this unique program. Even though it was an athletic program, it was about so much more than just tennis. When I first began coaching the Shooting Stars travel basketball team, I decided to model the team after the Say Yes to Tennis program — to use the program not only to coach basketball but to be a ministry as well. I decided that as a coach, I had the opportunity to do what my mentors had done for me — to serve as a role model. My agenda was to try to live a Christian example in front of the kids as opposed to just sitting them down for Bible study and forcing them to digest principles without showing them in action in their own lives. I'd experienced the latter approach in my own childhood and knew it was rarely effective.

I remember one particular road trip where our reservations had been messed up by the hotel. Even though we were more than a little grumpy and tired after being crammed into a minivan for seven hours, the group with me needed to see me keep my cool and not raise my voice. So instead of banging my fist on the counter (like I wanted to) and making a scene, I politely asked the desk clerk to check her computer again.

I wanted them to understand it's OK to speak to someone in a courteous manner in order to get things done. I wanted them to know we all make mistakes. I tried to show them how to live without allowing our ego to get out of control and stooping to the pettiness that often comes with it. I wanted to show them by my actions that if a referee blew an important call, I didn't fly off the handle and start throwing curse words around a gym full of young boys. Like many coaches, my frustration with refs probably gets higher than I care to admit, but I was conscious of never letting my emotions get out of control and saying something inappropriate or disrespectful in front of them.

It was crucial for the kids around me to also see that whenever I spoke to my wife, I spoke with respect. That I opened car doors for her and helped her into her seat when we sat down for dinner in a restaurant. That even when we disagreed about something, we talked about it civilly and respectfully.

These might seem like small, ordinary things, but for boys who might not have grown up with a father, they were huge. It was important that they see my wife and me model a successful marriage relationship on a day-to-day level.

In my experience, kids in single-parent situations often don't know how to deal with authority figures. They seem to fall into two categories — belligerent or timid. It's as if they either want to prove their manhood by getting in your face with aggression or don't want to deal with you at all. I don't give them a chance to be belligerent because I know kids are naturally reactionary — if I give them something to react to, they'll do just that. Conversely, if they're timid or shy, I try to instill confidence in them by showing them how important it is to make eye contact and project one's voice to communicate confidently. I let them know it's OK, and even good, to hold their heads high.

It's not easy to gain the trust of kids today — especially those from single-parent homes. So it's important to establish a foundation of trust with them that clearly says, *I am here for you. I want to help you.* That means you have to prove to them you are worthy of their trust, so that once they do trust you, you can effectively get involved in other areas of their lives. But it's a fine line when it comes to mentorship because, on the one hand, you want them to feel comfortable with you but, on the other hand, not so comfortable that they feel they can slack off. Which is why I always try to remind myself that I'm there to mentor them first and coach them second. But what I'm not there to do is to be their friend.

Traveling as a group also served as an opportunity for me and my coaches to teach beyond basketball. So we tried to make every trip be about more than the sport. If we were in Memphis for a game, for example, we made it a point to go to the National Civil Rights Museum at the old Lorraine Motel. It was important for them to understand that while basketball might have gotten them out of Akron, there was much more to see than just another court. I wanted their lives to be enriched in as many ways as possible.

Ultimately, I wanted the guys to use basketball to become productive members of society. The sport itself can't magically transform a slacker into this profile, but I believe that with some hard work, a person can use this sport to help get them there. Now I hope this hasn't come off like I'm trying to suggest I'm some sort of saint. Like everyone else, I've made plenty of mistakes. Despite my best intentions, there were moments when I lost my cool, screamed at a ref, or disagreed with my wife.

But despite my slipups, the boys were able to see the strength of my faith. I didn't talk about it much, but I always showed it to them to the best of my ability at any given moment. I felt it was more important and effective to see it played out, so I chose to show them my faith in action. To not deal in doubt or negativism; to be hardworking and humble; to take care of those around me. Am I perfect? By no means. But I held up a standard to them, and to this day, I need to do my best to keep to that standard. And if I fall short, I need to be honest and say, "I blew it."

For them to be the best, I had to be the best, so I coached those boys with all my heart, and in turn, they played their hearts out. When it became clear I was indeed a mentor, entrusted with the consecrated responsibility of teaching and showing these kids right from wrong, I realized I would have to take the focus off of winning. Instead, I chose to teach them about being good teammates, about collaborating and cultivating skills as individuals and as a group. Our motto was, "If you teach them how to play, the winning will take care of itself."

That meant focusing on teaching them the fundamentals — not only how to dribble and shoot but also how to move without the ball, how to stay with their man on defense or box out their man for a rebound — the nuances involved in becoming a great basketball player. The difference between a good team and a great team is the attention paid to the details. That is true for basketball as much as it is for life, and by the time they started playing games, my kids' skill levels were well above average for kids that age.

But more than their individual skills (not to mention the out-of-this-world ability Bron was already beginning to demonstrate), what I really loved about the Shooting Stars was their cohesiveness as a team. I loved that even though Bron was clearly the most skilled player on whatever floor he walked onto, it wasn't just him and some nameless sidekicks. The Shooting Stars were a team, first and foremost. But if I allow myself some credit in helping mold those attributes, then I have to say an inspiration to really preach teamwork and selflessness was something mentored to me. And the coach who taught me to do this was none other than the legendary John Wooden.

Now to be clear, I never met Coach John Robert Wooden, let alone played for him or coached under him. For those of you who may not know, Coach Wooden was the longtime head basketball coach at UCLA, where he won eleven NCAA championships and went down in history as one of the greatest, if not *the* greatest, basketball coach of all time.

But even though I never had the chance to meet him personally, Coach Wooden was a key figure in my development as a coach. Today I'm known as a basketball coach, but you must remember that when I first started coaching the Shooting Stars, my knowledge of the game really was no deeper than that of any other casual fan. Sure, I could play the game a little bit myself, and like most fans I'd act like a know-it-all and complain about a coach's strategy when I watched a game on TV. But when it was time to give the boys technical instruction, it soon became apparent to me that I was out of my depth. Even with eleven-year-olds.

As I began to search for some instruction, one of the first things I did was turn to Coach Wooden's books. One reason I was drawn to him was the fact that I knew he was a Christian. And I also knew that by reputation he was one of the greatest coaches in the game's history. Growing up, UCLA was my favorite team, and I watched them every chance I got. So between his faith and his success, Coach Wooden seemed like a great place to start.

I made it a goal to read every single one of his books. I soaked up his methodology as if I were in some kind of self-imposed private class. I told myself that readers are leaders and had faith that an immersion into Coach Wooden's approach would not only serve me well but be the best thing for my players too.

Much of what Coach Wooden taught has stayed with me over the years, but one saying in particular really left a mark — so much so that I wrote it down on a piece of paper and taped it to the dashboard of my car. At the time, I was driving the kids to many different places for practices and games, so we were on the road a lot, and to me it was important that this insight was always front and center. It read: *Talent is God-given, be thankful; fame is man-given, be humble; conceit is self-given, be careful.* I would come back to this again and again with the boys, especially with the success that would come to them, to us, like an avalanche. Like Coach Wooden with his team, I wanted my boys to really grasp the fact that they were part of something bigger than themselves, and that the process didn't begin and end with them.

Coach Wooden also helped recast my definition of competition, which I made sure my boys understood too. In some ways, people have a tough time seeing the nature of competition as an innately Christian principle. But as John Wooden wrote and coached, competition has nothing to do with the other team; rather, it's about how one's own group comes together to work toward a common goal. That, according to Coach Wooden, is the real definition of competition and the one we chose to focus on as a team. It's not about who you're playing *against*; it's about who you're playing *with*.

Coach Wooden's hyperfocus on the power of collaboration informed so much of the way I coach and, in turn, what my boys picked up from me. He made it clear that for the group to be successful, each individual has to be willing to sacrifice for the group. "I would rather have a good player who makes other players great than a great player," he wrote, which was another brilliant insight that stuck with me. With a player like LeBron James in the mix, it was sometimes hard to make that point. I'd have to remind them that sometimes you're Batman and sometimes you're Robin — and that *both* roles matter significantly as long as everyone stays the course. And ultimately, our team's success was based on how they played as a group. I was not going to be able to do it alone, nor were they. Not even Bron.

When Bron, Dru III, and Sian were seniors at St. Vincent-St. Mary, we were asked to play at the Staples Center, the home of the Los Angeles Lakers. For most basketball coaches, that would have been the ultimate thrill, but I had another idea. While I usually don't make special requests, in this instance I broke character and told the game organizers I wanted to play at Pauley Pavilion instead. Bron at the time was the most famous high school basketball player ever, and everyone desperately wanted to get games with us. So I put in a request for Pauley Pavilion, and not too long afterward, I found myself coaching on the same floor my mentor Coach Wooden once patrolled. Some of the kids were disappointed they didn't get to experience the glitz and glamour of playing at the home of the Lakers, but to me Pauley Pavilion was much more appropriate. The kids might have loved Kobe Bryant and Shaquille O'Neal, but whether or not they realized it, it was Coach Wooden who had helped teach them the game.

The lesson is that not everyone has the chance to be in direct contact with a great mentor, but the key to experiencing effective and inspiring mentorship, no matter who or where you are, is to know how to identify potential mentors. By reading Coach Wooden's books, I felt like I did know him personally, and, more importantly, his insights armed me spiritually and practically on my own journey to become the kind of coach (and man) I wanted to be.

This is such a critical lesson for people growing up in difficult circumstances. I can't fault a kid who grew up in poverty for saying, "I never had any support." Just as I can't fault a kid who grew up without a father for saying, "I never got any leadership." But I can encourage them to understand there are other ways to find that support, to find that direction.

Yes, every kid should be able to have that support at home or, at best, in his or her extended family, but as we know, too many don't. Which is why we need to remind them that they can find support from others — even from a book. That even though someone isn't in your family or from your hood, or doesn't even seem to share any experiences with you, they can still help change your life for the better.

Remember, Coach Wooden was a white man who grew up on a farm in Indiana and started coaching in the 1930s. I am an African-American man from East Liverpool, Ohio, who was a manager for a food company at the same age Coach Wooden had already won a national title. Outside of our faith, on the surface there doesn't appear to be much of a connection. But as I hope you're gathering from these words, I credit much of whatever success I've had to him.

And while I've been talking about helping young people find the right role models, this is a lesson that applies to *all* ages. Remember, I was a middle-aged man when Coach Wooden became my role model. I had a family and all the responsibilities that come with it. I even had my pension at ConAgra in sight. That's a stage in life when a person can easily fall into the trap of believing they've figured everything out. But the truth is, no matter how many children we have under our roofs or how many years we've spent in our vocations, we've never even come close to figuring it out. There is always someone out there who can teach us something of value, who can show us how to make our journeys a little bit easier. And that's as true for a fifteen-year-old as it is a forty-year-old.

Remember, just because you haven't had obvious role models physically present in your life doesn't mean you must move through life alone. There are all kinds of sources you can turn to for advice, through the words of artists, authors, business leaders, preachers, coaches, educators, and beyond. Mentorship can come from anyone. There is wisdom everywhere. Just be bold enough to seek it.

Another coach who helped teach me the game was Keith Dambrot, currently the head coach of the men's basketball team at the University of Akron. I first met Coach Dambrot when Dru was in seventh grade. By that time, there was no doubt in Dru's mind that he wanted to be a basketball player, despite being on the short side for his age. He was incredibly focused on improving as a player, so I'd often take him to clinics and camps in the Akron area. But instead of just dropping him off, I'd stick around and watch. Not only did I do this to root for him as a father, but I was also eager to hear and see what other coaches were doing.

We wound up at a camp run by Coach Dambrot, and he and Dru quickly forged a wonderful relationship. I think one of the reasons they bonded was because both of them were short and had an incredible work ethic. I think Coach Dambrot knew what it was like to be a short guy in a big man's game and respected how Dru handled it.

At the time, Coach Dambrot wasn't coaching, but the following year he accepted a coaching job at St. Vincent-St. Mary. Today, STVM is known throughout the country as a basketball powerhouse, thanks in large part to the success of the teams we had with Bron, as well as some of the success we've been fortunate to experience in recent years.

STVM, before Coach Dambrot, was probably best known as

a football school. But he helped change that perception, building a program around an aggressive and disciplined style of basketball. It suited Dru well, and I could tell he wanted to play for Coach Dambrot at STVM.

BIG DECISIONS, BIG IMPACT

Since we're talking about St. Vincent-St. Mary, I want to address how the boys and I ultimately ended up at that school. It was an extremely controversial development at the time, and people continue to talk about it in Akron to this day.

A year after Dru first started working out with Coach Dambrot, I had joined the staff at Buchtel High School, a predominately African-American public school that had long been (and still is) one of the basketball powerhouses in Akron. Though nothing had been promised, it was expected that when Dru, Bron, Sian, and Willie were ready for ninth grade, they would join me at Buchtel.

They had been playing together since they were eleven years old and considered themselves an inseparable team. Wherever one of them went, *all* of them were going to go. And everyone (myself included) assumed it would be Buchtel. With me already on the bench as an assistant coach, everything seemed lined up, and besides, for any inner-city African-American kid who could play ball, Buchtel was where you went. That's just how it was.

In the fall of Dru III's eighth-grade year, I took him to the preseason open-gym sessions at Buchtel. I thought it was great because it gave him the chance to play with good competition and let the coaches begin to get an appreciation for his game. But after a few sessions, something seemed to be nagging at him. I didn't know what it was, but I could tell he was unsettled. Then one day he worked up the nerve to spit it out.

"Dad," he said, "they're not going to give me a chance here."

"What do you mean?" I asked. "I haven't heard anyone talking like that."

"They won't say it to you, but they think I'm too small to play here," he replied. "Some of the other coaches have been making little comments to me. They want Bron and Sian, but they're not interested in me. I'm never going to get a fair shot."

I tried to argue that he'd get a fair shot, if not at first, then eventually. But Dru was adamant that it wasn't the right place for him. "I'm not going to Buchtel, Dad," he proclaimed.

And then he delivered a shocker.

"I want to go to St. Vincent-St. Mary," he declared with all the certainty in the world. "Coach Dambrot trusts me. I'm going to get a fair shake there. I've put in too much work to get counted out before I even get a chance."

I respected what he had to say because I understood going somewhere you don't feel wanted can be tough. When Dru told Bron, Sian, and Willie about his decision, they decided they would follow him to STVM. Part of it was because Dru was a leader, and the passion with which he spoke about Coach Dambrot and his program was contagious. But I believe it really came down to the fact that they weren't ready to part with one another — as teammates or friends. They wanted to keep playing together, and they would — even though they would catch a lot of heat for that decision.

You see, the choice to enroll at St. Vincent-St. Mary instead of Buchtel was about way more than them picking one high school over another. People in the community saw it not as a matter of schooling or even competing basketball programs but more as a matter of race. Buchtel was overwhelmingly black, and STVM was overwhelmingly white. So when the "Fab Four" picked STVM, the African-American community immediately called them traitors and sellouts.

And I can understand the disappointment. Even at that age, the kids were already local legends on the basketball scene. And while LeBron's star hadn't yet ascended to the heights soon to come, people already understood he was something special. The African-American community wanted him to bring his talents to Buchtel, so to see him and his boys leave a black school in the hood for a middle-class white school had to sting.

But the fact is, these kids had made up their minds and were going to STVM, whether or not the community liked it. Of course, that decision made my own presence at Buchtel a bit uncomfortable, as you can imagine. I finished out the season and then resigned from the staff, but Coach Dambrot quickly offered me a position on his bench.

While the controversy surrounding the kids' decision was at times painful, there was very little looking back. Personally, I was excited by how much I was learning about the game from Coach Dambrot. He had already been a Division I college coach at Central Michigan University, so it was invaluable for me to be able to watch him up close.

Coach Dambrot had a more detailed and structured approach to coaching than any I had been exposed to — one that provided me with a map I could follow on my own journey as a coach. While Coach Wooden guided me in the area of integrity and purpose, Coach Dambrot spoke to the practical elements of coaching the game. The trickle-down effect of this mentorship was invaluable, because the more I learned, the more my boys would learn, and the more they knew, the better they did.

In fact, some of what we still do today at St. Vincent-St. Mary hasn't changed much from the days of Dambrot's system. I've added to it, but the basic foundation hasn't changed. Why should it? It has been proven to work. And the proof is in the pudding because the one thing that coaches always say to me about our kids who go on to play in college is that our guys are prepared; they're ready to play. They have a better understanding of how the game is played, and I like to believe Keith Dambrot was key in laying down that foundation.

But the truth is that those boys taught me as much as I, or Coach

Dambrot, taught them. They were a group of strangers who just magically bonded, as if they were meant to come together this way. The love they shared for the game was grounded in their love for one another, and as such, they showed me the power of true camaraderie. By being such a close-knit group, they were one another's mentors too. I cherished seeing them become each other's role models, knowing firsthand the way negative peer pressure can play out, having succumbed to it in my own college career. I felt somehow redeemed as I saw them rise up collectively. My goal became to make them value one another more than they did the game, to seek the mentorship in one another. They played their hearts out for themselves, but they did it even more so for one another. There was a sharing going on. Despite the onslaught of criticism that came their way for picking St. Vincent-St. Mary, they made it as a group and stuck together like a family. As Sian Cotton poignantly once said, "You play your heart out for your family."

SUPPORT AND GUIDANCE PAYOFF

I believe this presence of mentorship helped mold Bron into the superstar he is today. Bron has obviously been blessed with incredible physical abilities, but there's no way to overlook that he was short-changed in other areas. Growing up, Dru always had me; Sian had his father, Lee; Willie had his older brother. But Bron lacked a father figure to latch on to. As a youngster, he and his mother moved around constantly — to the point that sometimes they didn't know if they'd have a place to lay their heads that night. And during the periods they did have a steady place to stay, it often wasn't the type of place you'd want it to be. Certainly not for a child. On many nights, Bron would have to fall asleep to the sounds of loud music, the wailing of sirens, or, worse yet, gunshots.

Growing up with a sense of rootlessness also made it challenging to lock down friendships, and despite his talent, humor, and upbeat disposition, Bron often felt disconnected and lost. Fortunately, he had enough positive influences to help turn the awful sounds that once filled his childhood reality into those of dribbling basketballs and the powerful *swoosh* of his own dunks.

No matter how gifted Bron has always been, perhaps more than any other player I've ever coached, his ultimate strength as a player was fueled by the love and support his friends and teammates provided to him. Even today, when you watch Bron play in the NBA, it's evident just how much love there is between him and his teammates. This may seem like a trite observation — "Well, of course they love him; he's the best player on the team," you may say. But think about it. Just being the best player on a team doesn't always translate into being beloved. Quite the opposite, in fact. Or think of your own experiences. Did you always love, and feel loved by, the best player on whatever team you played for? Probably not.

But this need to create a true bond — both on and off the court — has always been at the heart of Bron's success.

While the boys, my wife, and I helped give Bron a sense of family and stability, other individuals helped build him up as a young man too. When he was a nine-year-old fourth grader, his mother sent him to live with his Pee Wee football coach and family, the Walkers, until she could get herself back on her feet. They were a disciplined family that demanded the same from Bron. He was expected to wake up early, carry out his chores, and take pride in any sense of responsibility that came his way. Just like the rest of the Walker kids, Bron was expected to help wash the dishes, sweep the floor, scrub countertops, and take out the trash. The family gave him a dose of stability that laid the groundwork for the person he would eventually become.

And ultimately, he found his essence, his sense of place and self, on the court. On that road, he was savvy enough to recognize the power of selecting mentors and directed a lot of his energy toward emulating them. When his mother found a place for them to live, he transformed his bedroom into a veritable shrine to his mentors, among them Michael Jordan, Kobe Bryant, and Allen Iverson, their pictures plastered on his walls like a wallpaper of his own future intentions.

There's a saying, "People come into your life for a reason, a season, or a lifetime." Given the nature of things, mentors don't stay in their position as mentors forever, but I like to think Bron and the rest of the boys will always see me as their mentor. Romeo Travis, who joined the team after the rest of the boys were already at STVM, has said he would not know where he would be had he not met me, which, of course, means the world to me. I know they still love and respect me, and I feel if I needed anything from any of them today, they'd be there at the drop of a hat.

Bron, for example, still entrusts me with the use of his name for some of the camps and clinics I run on his behalf, which in today's brand-obsessed world is no small thing, which is not to say we're on the phone every night discussing strategy or his last game. No, there are folks who are way more qualified than I am for that part of his life right now. But I know our connection runs deep. At the end of it all, to hear someone like Bron, who has accomplished so much while overcoming so much, say, "You're my role model" — well, for me that's the ultimate. To know I've had a major impact on who he is.

And to be clear, I'm not talking about Bron's jump shot or how he plays defense. My impact on Bron's life can't be quantified in X's and O's. Instead, if he's taken anything of lasting value from my mentorship, I want it to be how to carry himself through life as a man, husband, and father. I remember being in a restaurant with the team after the game we played at the Palestra, a legendary school gym in Philadelphia, during Bron's senior year. He walked over to the table where my wife and I sat and proudly announced that one day he wanted to be just like Mrs. Joyce and me. And now he is a loving husband and a doting father. He treats his wife with respect and love and is there, day in and day out, for his children. And I like to believe he learned a lot of that from watching us.

Unfortunately, when we look at a superstar like Bron today, we tend to think they were self-made. But the truth is that to reach the heights Bron has reached takes a great deal of support, mentorship, and role modeling, especially when a person has to overcome such difficult circumstances. So many people have helped Bron along his journey — from his mother, Gloria, to our family, the Walkers, the Cottons, his teammates over the years, and folks like Maverick Carter, who transitioned from being a teammate to being one of his closest advisers.

Bron's example is just another reason we need to debunk the myth that "real men" always go at it alone. A youngster who grows up believing that will never receive the guidance they so desperately need. To say nothing of those at different stages of life who still desperately need a guiding hand or encouraging words.

Whenever you think you've accomplished something on your own, you're fooling yourself. If you don't acknowledge the individuals who have helped you along the way, you are not recognizing how the world's system works. Everyone who has ever been successful at anything has had the help of someone else. That's just the nature of humanity — a gift really.

As a mentor, having the opportunity to pour your life into someone else is a supreme kind of responsibility and opportunity, and you need to cherish it. And as a student, you need to always remember that once you stop learning, you essentially start dying. You have to always hold on to the belief that life is a journey that stretches out into an unknown future, which means you can never just stop and kick up your feet. You have to keep moving and growing, and one of the greatest ways to do that is by taking cues from the teachers around you. Look around, and you will see they are everywhere.

CHAPTER 4

Use the Game; Don't Let the Game Use You

Difficulties mastered are opportunities won.

Winston Churchill

I'm about to board a plane with my wife to watch Dru (who isn't so little anymore) play professional basketball in Germany. He's the point guard for the EWE Oldenburg Baskets. Dru, the kid who assumed the coaches and players at Buchtel High School would never give a player his size a chance and chose another school just to avoid that reality. Dru, with the skinny little arms. Dru, the short kid who used to be called "mascot" and "pixie" by small-minded people who couldn't imagine small basketball players. Dru, who had to contend with the reality of being compared to players with the size and skill set of a LeBron James. Dru, the barely four-foot-one kid who had a pull-up bar installed on the doorpost of his childhood bedroom, where he'd hang from his arms, hoping to lengthen his body for more height.

It's funny, because I distinctly remember his dresser being right near that pull-up bar, and on top of it was a globe of the world — which I like to believe was a kind of foreshadowing of what was to come for my hardworking son, who perhaps intuitively knew he would one day get to see and experience the world via basketball.

As much of a miracle as it was to witness a player like Bron flourish into his fullest expression, it was just as extraordinary (perhaps even more so) to watch a player like Dru, despite his challenges, truly come into his own as well. So what trait did two best friends and teammates have in common, despite their extreme physical differences? One word: *volition*. They shared the dream of not only becoming the best basketball players they could be but also making that dream come true *on their terms.*

"Guys were getting bigger and I wasn't growing, so I had to add something else to my game," Little Dru once told me in a matter-of-fact tone when I complimented him on what a great shooter he had become. Dru was trying to be nonchalant about it, but I saw it as a testament to the fact that he was determined to realize his dream by working with his God-given circumstances. At no point did he turn his back on his goal; I don't think it ever crossed his mind. Instead of surrendering to the preconceptions of ballplayers having to be a certain size, he found a way to excel at the game in a manner that made sense for him.

"He wasn't always the biggest, the fastest, or the cutest, but man, he was tough as nails," Bron once joked about his close friend. And he was right. That little man showed the heart of a warrior on the court, proving to everyone around him that hard work, determination, and keeping your heart fixed on the dream could be enough to defy just about any odds.

When Coach Dambrot first met Dru, he said my son showed a skill level and work ethic that was well above average for a seventh grader. I knew Dru was a worker, but I appreciated hearing that from a seasoned (and more objective) coach. While many other coaches gave Dru the feeling he'd have to grow taller to play—which only helped heighten whatever insecurity my son may have harbored about his size—Keith made it a point to show Little Dru that size meant nothing to him as a coach. His belief in my son relayed the most important message—*good basketball is good basketball,* no matter what the circumstances may be. This philosophy became rooted in Dru and influenced his approach as a committed, passionate player. Coach Dambrot was intent on putting my son in a position to be successful, because, like me, he didn't want to see Dru fall victim to the perceptions of what a good basketball player was *supposed* to be. Like me, he wanted to see Dru shine. And Dru shone by using the game rather than letting the game use him. He refused to abide by the conventional wisdom of the game that says you have to be a certain height to play it.

FAMILY MATTERS

But size was not the only challenge Dru faced. The fact that he was my son — a coach's son — was also something he and I had to contend with. I will never forget driving a bunch of kids around Ohio one weekend when I overheard one of them say to Dru, "The only reason you're even playing is because your dad is the coach." I felt my skin turn hot and the blood in my chest start to pump.

But I would be lying if I said it was the only time, either to my face or behind my back, someone suggested Dru was playing only because his dad was his coach. My way of debunking that myth was to work Dru *even harder* than the other players. If people wanted to think Dru was getting a free ride, then I would make it clear to anyone watching that if anything, Dru's path was going to be even more challenging. In time, people got the message. But being that tough as a coach also began to affect my relationship with Dru as his father. This was especially true when Dru and the Fab Four were just starting at St. Vincent-St. Mary.

There were times when I questioned myself: *Am I taking it too far? Is this the best thing for him?* I was relentless about building him as a player, not only spending extra hours with him at the gym as he took jump shots and worked on his dribble but also spending hours at home watching tapes and discussing strategy. I wanted him to feel in his bones that he earned every single moment of court time he got solely because he worked hard for it. He and everyone around him needed to know his success as a player had nothing to do with being my son. His achievements were built into his passion for the game and his personal will to ensure he would master it. And master it he did — as evidenced during the last game of his freshman year of high school.

It was the Division III state championship game against Jamestown Greeneview. The last time STVM earned the title "state champion" was 1984. The game was held at the Value City Arena in Columbus, with more than 13,000 excited high school basketball fans in attendance. The stakes were high and the pressure immense, especially for a freshman.

As Dru was warming up before the game, I noticed some of the Greeneview fans in the stands, their faces painted in red and blue, laughing at him because of his size. They were shouting out taunts, like, "Hey, have you reached puberty yet?" or "Hey, this is a high school game. No fifth graders allowed!" It wasn't vicious stuff, but it could have affected his focus, and I prayed he wasn't hearing any of it. And if he was, I hoped his focus would block out all the negativity.

After several minutes, we were down by three points when Coach Dambrot decided to bring Dru into the game. "*Diminutive* would be a mild understatement," quipped the radio announcer as Dru stripped off his sweats and strode onto the court. "He's generously listed as five foot two, but I think everyone's under the consensus he's closer to four foot eleven."

After a couple of possessions, Dru found himself alone behind the three-point line on the left side of the court. He caught a bounce pass and without hesitation nailed a three-pointer.

Nothing but net.

The crowd roared as the announcer chuckled. "Wow. You almost couldn't see him shoot it" — implying that the ball was bigger than Dru's head.

Moments later, Dru got the ball at the top of the key and drilled another three-pointer.

Nothing but net again.

A few possessions later, Bron took a pass just beyond the arc, turned toward Dru, and fired a pass. Again, my "too-small" boy launched another three.

Nothing but net.

The first two might have been flukes, but after the third, it was obvious something was happening. As much as I wanted to run over and give Dru a hug, I resisted the temptation, lest I somehow alter his rhythm.

As the first half wound down, he got the ball in the left corner again. One of Jamestown's big men ran toward him, his long arms raised in an attempt to block the shot, but Dru got it off just in time.

Again, nothing but net.

In the second half, Jamestown keyed on Dru, sending a defender flying at him every time he caught the ball. But it didn't matter. He nailed another three to start the half, and then another. Followed by one more.

Soon we had the game in control and ended up winning by almost twenty points. Dru clearly made the difference in the game, finishing with 21 points, hitting an improbable seven for seven three-pointers.

The crowd had come out that day to see the young prodigy Bron work his magic (which he did) — so you can imagine how blown away everyone (on both sides of the stands!) was when Dru stole the show. Instead of letting basketball dictate how he would perform, he showed up to play basketball with the spirit of an unstoppable fighter. As Sian put it later, "He didn't want anyone to say anything about his size 'cause he had the confidence to play against anyone. He would just do it a different way." And just like that, in an instant, the smallest boy on the court became the giant in the room.

After they won, Bron came over to Dru and squeezed him with a sense of love and admiration that said, *I knew you could.* Imagine that. You are barely five feet tall and someone with as much stature and talent as Bron stands fully in awe of you. That, to me, is the definition of playing on your terms. Bron scooped him up and held him high, almost like he was telling the crowd, *Look at the size of this guy now!* When the trophy was given to the Fighting Irish of St. Vincent-St. Mary, it was Dru who got to hold it high as the crowd roared.

Reflecting on it later, one journalist said of Dru's three-point barrage, "It was a transcendent moment — one that most people there will always remember." Never again would anyone dare to doubt his skill or make asinine comments about him being my son. No, from that moment on, the larger world began to understand what we already knew in our home: Dru could play. And he was going to keep playing until somebody told him he couldn't. A moment, I'm proud to say, that still hasn't happened. The lesson here is simple: Just as limitations can sometimes be self-imposed, so also are our own abilities to powerfully transcend them. And sometimes the very thing that seems to stop us on our path toward achievement is precisely that which catalyzes our ability to get there. If you take anything from this story, let it be this: A challenge seen in the right light can be like fuel for triumph.

OPPORTUNITIES ARE LOW-HANGING FRUIT

My son's determination to use the sport to his advantage ultimately landed him a position on a professional basketball team in Germany. Even though I know Dru's dream as he grew up was to play in the NBA, I couldn't be prouder of where he's wound up in his career. Yes, he might not be making NBA-caliber money, but he's definitely earning an income three times as high as most people who have been out of college for several years. Not only is he able to support his family comfortably; he also gets an added bonus of being able to experience other cultures and environments. His daughter speaks German (he and his wife are still working on it), which, if you've ever heard it spoken, is no small feat. He's able to move freely in a different culture and see both America and the world from a different vantage point — all of which colors and broadens his perspective. He lives in a world surrounded by new flavors and stimulation, which he would never have been able to partake of had he not become determined to use the game on his own very specific terms.

When I advise him, I remind him that the "game" is always changing, and the game for him now has to include a big-picture plan — not just one that serves him but also his family. What happens when the basketball years come to an end (which they inevitably do)? What will he take from it? Will he have saved enough? I always tell him that if he understands the value of money and keeps this fundamental concept in its proper place, recognizing money is there to help him live a life where he's not always looking for his next meal, then he'll be OK. All of these questions will have to play into how my son and the rest of those young men use the game — so they don't get used. It's about understanding every aspect of every opportunity at every moment — past, present, and future.

Too many athletes have allowed the game to use them, finding out they were recruited to make money for their college institutions. They end up leaving without a degree or job prospects or skills because they were funneled into dead-end majors that provided no real future. Instead of taking control of their own destiny, they allowed themselves to be swept along with the current.

For a lot of younger players, the game has already used them up before they leave high school. Many never reach college because of ineligibility. They don't effectively apply themselves in the classroom, so they are left with few options. I've had to emphasize to many of my players the importance of being a student-athlete. I remind them of the standard they have to reach to qualify for a scholarship and how difficult it is to get one, even if they reach the standard, because there are only slightly more than 4,400 Division I basketball scholarships available for the entire world. I impress on them that the odds of getting a scholarship are very slim and that if they get one they're in a select group so it behooves them to stay academically focused. Even though I'm a staunch believer in the concept of dedicating one's self to the pursuit of one's goals, I also believe it's imperative to diversify in life and cast a wide net, which will only help to broaden your horizons as you move through life.

The takeaway for the rest of us is to think beyond the current moment. Where are you in the current game of career and family, and where do you hope to be in ten years? Twenty years? Your destiny is shaped by your decisions, not by your current circumstances.

THE SPORTS PARADOX

I remember talking to a guy who was trying to become Bron's agent. He had primarily dealt with football players in the National Football League, and he said something that stuck with me: "Seventy percent of these guys finish their stints in the NFL and walk away with no money. Their careers are so short and we are so shortsighted that we don't even see the built-in problem in the model we've built." This is exactly why I find it crucial to help a kid understand that when it comes to sports, the moment of opportunity is very small. It is a tiny window of time and circumstances that one needs to not only identify but also jump on quickly.

One of the things I'm proudest of as a coach was hearing Bron once say to a reporter, "The number one thing Coach Dru taught us was to use the game of basketball and not let the game of basketball use us. That set us up for life after the game of basketball in a way I can't explain." If I taught these kids nothing else, it gives me profound joy and satisfaction to know I was able to relay this truth.

And while owning a team is likely the ultimate extension of one's professional basketball career, I realize most players who pass through my program will never get a chance to realize that dream. But even for a player who never will advance past the college ranks, there are so many ways to parlay the game of basketball into opportunities that will bring lasting value to their lives. A great example of someone who put this principle into practice is Maverick Carter, who today serves as Bron's manager. Maverick was a senior at STVM when Bron and Dru were freshmen and was a very good player. Even though Maverick left the University of Akron after one year of college basketball, he figured out a way to use the game to elevate his life and the lives of those around him. Because of his friendship with Bron in high school, Maverick was able to build that relationship into a business partnership with him that has proved incredibly fruitful for both of them. As the president of the LRMR marketing firm, Maverick has not only created a multitude of endorsement and media opportunities for Bron but also paved the way for relationships with Warren Buffet, Nike's Phil Knight, rap superstar Jay-Z, and countless other movers and shakers. *Inc.* magazine put Maverick on their list of the "30 top entrepreneurs under the age of 30," and as I write this, news media are reporting that Bron's stake in Beats by Dre headphones (a stake Maverick helped negotiate) just earned him $30 million after the company was recently sold to Apple. And perhaps most importantly, LRMR has helped many people from Akron get opportunities they otherwise would have never experienced. So even though the seventeen-year-old Maverick had his heart set on being a pro player, his postathletic career is a textbook example of how to successfully leverage the lessons learned from playing a team sport into a life of success.

Another person in Bron's orbit who is a great example of the "use the game; don't let the game use you" principle is his former coach on the Miami Heat, Erik Spoelstra. Coach Spoelstra was a decent college player at the University of Portland, where he started at point guard for four years. (A sad piece of trivia is that Coach Spoelstra was on the court during the 1990 game in which University of Marymount's Hank Gathers died from a heart attack.)

Despite Coach Spoelstra's success at the college level, he didn't get a shot at the NBA. Instead of giving up on the game, Erik played in

Germany, where he stayed for two years. After hurting his back, Coach Spo (as he's called) returned to the States, where he picked up a job as a video coordinator with the Miami Heat. Being a video coordinator is probably the lowest job there is on an NBA team, one that requires long, long hours without much pay. But instead of griping about the long hours, Coach Spo threw himself into the job, impressing Pat Riley, the Heat's head coach, with his dedication and work ethic. After a couple of years as video coordinator, Coach Spo was promoted to assistant coach and scout. And after four more years of hard work, he was promoted to become the team's head of scouting. In 2008, almost thirteen years after he joined the team, Coach Spo was appointed to be head coach after Coach Riley decided to step down. And after taking over the reins, Coach Spo led the team to four straight NBA Finals and established himself as one of the top coaches in the game.

Now I'm sure as a high schooler Coach Spo wanted to be an NBA player. But when it became clear it wasn't going to happen, he didn't give up on the game. Instead he threw himself into making himself valuable to the Miami Heat organization in whatever way he could. He paid his dues for years and years without complaint and took advantage of every opportunity he could to prove his worth. And by the time he was just forty, his hard work and dedication elevated him into one of the most desirable positions in professional sports.

Seeing how Dru III, Maverick, and Coach Spo have figured out how to elevate their lives through basketball is why I constantly preach "use the game" to my players. It can be a challenge to get that message through to them, though. If I've learned one thing in my years of coaching, it's that very few teenage boys have a realistic sense of where their basketball skills are going to take them.

EVERY MOVE COUNTS

One particular young man I coached almost turned down a college scholarship because he hoped a better one would come along.

He had an offer on the table from a perfectly good school, but he didn't want to take it because he was convinced (or perhaps someone else had convinced him) that a perennial top program like a North Carolina or a Duke was going to swoop in at the last minute and offer him a spot — a classic case of cutting off one's nose to spite one's face. Instead of getting into an argument with him, I decided to use some bottom-line logic. I calmly pointed out there are 340 Division I schools. "Let's do the math," I said. "There are 13 scholarships per school, and 13 x 340 is 4,420 scholarships for the entire world — and *you*, my friend, have one of them." I could see the wheels turning and could tell he was starting to see things with a bit more reason.

I tried to show him just how significant this really was. I wanted him to see he was set up to obtain a free education from basketball, which would give him the opportunity to use the game to his advantage. "You've done that," I said. "Let all the other stuff go. There is no better option. You can act like there is someone else who wants you, but you're better off being real about what's in front of you, what's right under your nose." I've learned that the best thing you can do as a coach is to help your players understand reality, and sometimes it means being brutally honest and laying it right out there for them to grasp.

"This is it," I said. "There is nobody else coming." I explained that if he were a "top 100" guy and walked away from this scholarship, there's a chance he might get another offer. "But you're not a top 100 guy," I said, leveling with him. "So let's be real about this. You've exceeded everyone's expectations because this college is the only one that has offered. Jump on this, and jump on it quickly."

I may have hurt his feelings in that instant, but I know for the long haul he was better served. A good coach isn't there to tell a young person what they want to hear but instead to lift the veil of delusion and encourage big-picture thinking based on truth. He took the scholarship, finished school with his degree, and is now playing professionally in Europe.

Another kid who played in my AAU program, C. J. McCollum,

earned a scholarship — this one to Lehigh University. When he started with me as a ninth grader, he was small and frail, like my sons, Dru and Cameron. Like my boys, C. J. loved the game and became a talented shooter, and by the time he got to his senior year of high school, he was about six foot one. At first he was adamant about not wanting to go to Lehigh, having had a great summer, with a slew of coaches coming out to watch him perform. All of a sudden, his name started cropping up, and he was getting a fair amount of buzz, so we moved on to a tournament in Las Vegas, where all the schools came out to watch him. I don't know if it was the pressure of all that or just a bad day, but he was so anxious that he didn't play well at all.

Despite that debacle, Lehigh still had their sights on C. J. — and wouldn't you know, this kid was still intent on declining their offer. I told his coach to tell him to go to Lehigh, where he'd see a world of opportunity open up to him. I wasn't trying to sound preachy, but I was fully aware of how true it was. Well, the kid ended up going to Lehigh, and much to the delight of all of us, not only did he make the All-Conference team as a freshman; he was voted Player of the Year as well. His team played in the NCAA tournament, and he scored 26 points against Kansas. Though his team lost, putting up 26 points against Kansas was nothing to scoff at. His sophomore and junior years at Lehigh were much like his first — Player of the Year honors, first team All-Conference — and in 2012, he scored 30 points in leading his team to an upset victory over the Duke Blue Devils in the NCAA tournament. It helped get the attention of the Portland Trail Blazers, who made him their lottery pick. Had he gone somewhere else, it wouldn't have happened. He wouldn't have experienced the unique opportunities Lehigh provided him.

The examples go on and on. I remember another guy from our program who struggled. He managed to get into St. Vincent-St. Mary but didn't perform well academically, not because he didn't try but because he had a learning disability that stood in his way. Yet, through some frustrating and trying times, we got him through. Complicating matters was the fact that his family was dysfunctional, with many of his relatives living the fast life. Despite those challenges, he wound up going to a junior college, which from my perspective was nothing short of a blessing straight from heaven. Yet after he had been on campus for only a few weeks, he called one day and said, "Coach, I can't take it. I don't like any of the people here and this place is boring. There's nothing to do, and all I can smell is cow manure."

I got so frustrated that I wanted to hang up on him. Didn't he understand he was preparing to squander an amazing opportunity? Didn't he know the only thing waiting for him back in Akron was the streets? His basketball talents had given him access to a larger world that his family situation and academic issues would have never otherwise allowed him to experience. But instead of laying into him, I swallowed hard and said, "Listen, I know you're out in the country, but you'll get used to it. Focus on the game, and don't let the other stuff get you down. Man, it's only two years of your life. Just stick it out." To his credit, he decided to stay for the first year. And during that time, he showed tremendous growth, both as a student and a ballplayer.

But sadly, he didn't go back for the second year. As I had feared, he chose the more familiar route and returned to the street life of his old neighborhood. He failed to realize that life ages you, that opportunities don't stop and wait for you to be ready. Instead they just find someone who is. Had he stayed in school, he would have been able to carve out a legacy — not just for him but also for his family — down the line. A college degree. A good job. An awareness of the world beyond the streets. This, to me, is the essence of using the game.

Take a moment to reflect on life and "the road not taken" on your own path. Don't do this out of regret, because after all, the past is unchangeable. However, the past is also full of insights for your future, and by taking a close look at the ways in which you could have more assertively reaped opportunity, you prepare yourself to do so down the line.

DARE TO VEER

The concept of using the game is not simply limited to athletics but applies to whatever "game" you play in life. It's a lesson I learned the hard way in my own career path, as I was never fully connected to my work or trajectory during my time in corporate America. I was just doing what I thought I was supposed to do. Blindly following the path that seemed "good enough." While it would be an exaggeration to say I wasted those years, I can now see I could have gained so much more from the experience if I had committed myself to it fully rather than just going through the motions.

When I was at ConAgra, one incident in particular sapped my passion for the job. After more than a decade on the job, I was still managing accounts instead of people, which in that corporate structure qualified me as a "first-level manager." But from time to time I would train new salespeople, showing them the ropes and how to deal with accounts. That sort of training made me a candidate for midlevel management.

To be honest, I was content at my present job, but as our family (and our bills) began to grow, I felt what I'm certain many fathers feel — I had to make a little more money to keep our finances afloat. Though I wasn't as career driven as some of my colleagues, things had been going well at work — I had consistently exceeded my quota and won multiple sales contests, which had afforded Carolyn and me some extravagant trips and prizes — and so I figured I was ready to move forward.

Moving into middle management required an employee to sit down with a company shrink who would assess management potential by using a set of psychological tests. I didn't think much of it and went to meet with the psychologist. But when I was informed of the results, I was irate. Based on what the psychologist said, the company opted to offer me a lateral move as a territory manager before moving me up to the position of a district manager, which I wanted.

The decision disappointed me. I'd already been unofficially training, to positive reviews, new salespeople. So how could they tell me I wasn't ready to do it officially? I already knew how to do all the things required of me in the more senior position. It made no sense to keep me stuck, and I let a lot of folks know I wasn't happy. But the company essentially said, in their corporate mumbo jumbo, "We ain't gonna budge."

At that time, the national sales manager at Hunt Wesson Foods, a division of ConAgra, was an African-American man who, I guess, had demonstrated he had the proper psychological makeup for management. Someone must have told him I was making noise about not getting promoted, and one day after a meeting, he pulled me aside and said, "Dru, I heard you were being an uppity nigger." I was shocked he said that to me, but I recovered and tried to defend myself. "Why should I take a lateral move?" I asked him. He kind of laughed, and when he did, I had to chuckle too. But in that very moment, I realized that corporate America was not and would never really be for me. I had not used the game. There were corporate rules I didn't quite understand, and by protesting, I wasn't being a team player. I wanted to do it my way and not their way.

And when I say "using the game," I'm not just talking about taking full advantage of the circumstances that surround your reality; I'm also talking about making sure they are the right kind of circumstances to begin with. You see, even though I resented the rules of the corporate hierarchy, the deeper issue was that I had absolutely zero desire to really be there at all. I managed to get ahead, inasmuch as the company would allow it, and was able to keep my family fed, which, of course, was the point of the whole thing. I was very grateful for all of it, but at the end of the day, I would ask myself, *What have I done that really matters?* It wasn't until I gave my undivided attention to the art of coaching that I felt I was even playing the game I wanted to play.

Even in my capacity as a full-time coach and business owner, I still had to face the reality that there will always be rules of the game I have to adhere to. The rules had changed from the corporate world to the coaching world; however, my goal now was to play the game and master it. This meant taking advantage of every opportunity given to me, drowning out the naysayers who believed I'd never be up to the task of being a head coach because I didn't come up the traditional way. It also meant respecting and accepting things I had no control over, such as a referee's call that could affect the outcome of a game.

The refs will make whatever call they deem appropriate, and my job is not to pass judgment on it or on them but to keep myself and my players focused on the game. If I get stuck on a bad call, so does my team, and at that point, I'm no longer a basketball coach; I'm a wrangler of emotions. It got to a point where I realized I was there to lead. My version of using the game had to be to step in as mentor and guide for these boys, and nothing — not even a lousy call by a ref — should stop me from doing just that. If we intend to use the game and not let the game use us, we need to come to terms with the fact that the game comes with rules, and those rules stipulate that referees make the calls. Period.

And it wasn't just that. I had to deal with a fair amount of bad press too. The media had a field day with me on a regular basis, claiming I was "just an AAU coach" and accusing me of often being in over my head. I had to teach myself to file these comments under "Things I Can't Control," just like the call of a ref, and to train my mind to regard such allegations as nothing more than someone's opinion. The moment I allow myself to get upset or even remotely disgruntled after hearing or reading such critiques, I am allowing the game to use me, becoming a pawn in the media's game of having to blame someone, of needing a scapegoat when my players do not perform. I have learned the hard lesson that players win games, and it's the coaches who lose them — it's just this funny double standard built into the culture of basketball. But to repeat, for me to use the game on my terms, such pettiness has to fall by the wayside, and my focus has to remain on leading my team.

There's no getting around the fact that sports are, by nature, competitive. However, this innate quality can sometimes subvert the whole endeavor by eclipsing the real reason any of us get involved — to grow as individuals, to develop passion through discipline, to collaborate. Using the game is about realizing the game is there to serve as a tool, a bridge even, to greater things. The moment we get caught up in the winning and losing, in the X's and O's, we've allowed ourselves to fall into the trap of being used by the game. By losing sight of our own agendas and caring solely about the win, we become exactly what the haters out there need to subsist — something to talk about, someone to scrutinize.

Even though losing the state championship during my first year as a head coach was a painful blow to the team and to me, it was also somehow a blessing in disguise. It showed us that we needed to redirect our focus, to stop caring about being No. 1 and instead put our collective energy toward a greater sense of balance. We needed that loss to shake up our consciousness, so that when the dust settled, our true values could again rise to the top. As their coach, I understood their skewed perspective started with me. I was the one who set the tone for how they would act and react out there. So it was on me to make sure they would come back to the court with a feeling of triumph that didn't hinge on wins or losses. I wanted them to feel victorious no matter what, with the certainty that despite the outcome of any one particular game, they were using the game as a whole to serve their life strategy.

Every moment of every single day, you have the opportunity to use to your advantage whatever "game" you are playing. Part of it is looking closely at your unique situation, as Dru did with his so-called size disadvantage. Part of it is knowing when to adjust your take on things, as Erik Spoelstra did on his way to becoming a head coach.

But all of it includes tapping into a big-picture worldview that serves you in that moment and beyond, so you aren't simply making decisions and moves that give you instant gratification but instead get you ready for winning the game of life.

Don't just be the player; master the game.

The original AAU team in 1996

My first travel team at the 11u AAU National Championships in Cocoa Beach

Northeast Ohio Shooting Stars team at the 15u AAU National Championships

Family photo in
summer of 2000

Cameron and me at the Luxor
Hotel in Las Vegas in July 2000

Thanksgiving 2009
with my daughters
India and Ursula

Carolyn and me at the
wedding of our close
friend's daughter in 2013

Dru and me after the 2001
State Championship game

Lebron and Dru III
during the District
Finals in Ohio, 2003

Newscom

Carolyn and me with LeBron at the NBA Draft
at Madison Square Garden in June 2003

At the 2003 NBA Draft
with my players

Encouraging the team
during a time-out

Time-out during the 2003 State Championship game

LeBron's uniform number being retired during a game in 2003

Coaching against our rival school Walsh Jesuit in my first year as head coach in 2002

Brandon Weems, LeBron, Dru, Sian Cotton, and Corey Jones in their senior year

LeBron, Romeo, Willie, Sian, Marcus Johnson, and Cameron with Dru at his wedding

LeBron and Dru on their graduation day

2009 State Championship team

2002 preseason fund-raising event for the Ronald McDonald House in Akron, Ohio. LeBron and Dru dribble a basketball for the last mile of a 5K race.

Akron Beacon Journal

2011 district champions who went on to win the state championship

The Fab Five and me at the Roundball Classic in Chicago

Our family at Cameron's wedding in July 2014

CHAPTER 5

Master the Art
of Discipline

> It is discipline, not just desire, which determines
> your destiny and mine.   *Charles Stanley*

When eleven-year-old LeBron James was asked what number he wanted to wear during the first year of his journey into travel basketball, his response was quick and to the point: "23" — which, of course, was a tribute to Michael Jordan, the basketball legend he aspired to emulate. This gesture, along with the multitudes of photographs ripped from dog-eared *Sports Illustrated* and *ESPN* magazines that covered his bedroom walls, were daily reminders of his own unflinching desire to one day be that great. He filled his periphery with images of proven talent that motivated him to strive.

However, these symbols served only as external punctuation to what this young boy really held inside, which was a burning, relentless determination to master the game. And somehow from a very early age, Bron intuitively knew his willfulness would only be one side of the coin, and that if he were to excel at the level of the great athletes he admired, he would have to tap into a force greater than his own desire — which I believe can be summed up in a single word: *discipline*. Bron became intent not only on mastering the art of basketball but on embracing the reality that the only way to do so is by mastering the art of discipline.

If we break down the word *discipline*, we see that the word *disciple* is front and center. When I looked up synonyms for *disciple*, the one that jumped out at me was *devotee*, which is exactly what I believe lies at the heart of discipline — an individual fiercely devoted to their passion and committed to showing up consistently so their passion can be transformed into a skill.

It seems to be a simple concept, and yet for some reason discipline is a missing ingredient in many people's lives. Even though it is the variable we can point to in the lives of those who are successful, it's a quality that people shy away from. Instead of trying to cultivate discipline, many of us react negatively to the word and, in doing so, perpetuate a distance from it. Maybe the only way to close the gap between ourselves and our sense of discipline is to recast its meaning in our lives.

When people think about the word *discipline*, they often put it in the context of a world of rules and edicts — a world where a strict disciplinarian doles out harsh punishments while laying down the law. This, however, is not the definition of discipline I aim to live by or to use as a coach. Having a sense of discipline is about understanding what your purpose in life really is and doing everything in your power to actualize it with an unwavering sense of excellence. When you think about it this way, discipline isn't really about rules; it's about standards.

Consider Bron's example again. He approached every aspect of basketball — whether in a state finals game or a preseason practice — as a matter of personal duty. I can attest to the fact that LeBron James has never taken for granted the raw talent he has been blessed with. Case in point: he missed only *one* practice from age ten through the end of his high school years. Remember, this was the same kid who once missed eighty days of class during a year in elementary school. Yet, by the time he was a preteen, he was completely dedicated to maximizing his gifts. To him, not being present was tantamount to not being committed, and I truly believe that if God hadn't given him the raw gifts he is known for, he would have still become one of the greatest basketball players of all time by using commitment and unyielding discipline as his compass to get there.

Later, when Bron was playing for the Cleveland Cavaliers and had already established himself as one of the game's greatest players, he still did daily workouts in the off-season, showing himself and everyone around him that you really do get back what you give. It was as if the court became his temple where he dutifully prayed morning, noon, and night; where he knew he had to be in order to be the best.

I think this may have been one of the reasons he was exasperated during his stint with the Cavs. He never articulated it, but I believe he felt he was working harder than everyone else, which can be immensely frustrating for someone who sets such high standards for himself. When the team had extended time off, he was in the gym bright and early on the very first day after taking a short weeklong break, whereas some of his teammates extended their vacations by another week, sometimes more, before heading back to training camp. He didn't have the patience for that, feeling somehow that every moment not on the court was one less moment to perfect his game. I think Bron would play ball whether or not he was getting paid, because it gives him a sense of foundation and a platform of constancy.

Conversely, I think one of the reasons his stint with the Heat was so successful is because he was surrounded by players who held the concept of discipline in similarly high regard. Teammate Ray Allen is often cited as one of the most disciplined players in the NBA. I remember when Ray first got to the Boston Celtics (his team before joining the Heat), a reporter asked him how he refined his God-given talent into being such a great shooter.

"That's an insult," replied Ray. "God couldn't care less whether I can shoot a jump shot."

Instead, Ray credited his skill as a shooter to his approach to the game. On the day of every game in his illustrious career, Ray follows the same routine:

- 11:30 a.m. to 1:00 p.m.: nap
- 2:30: eat a meal of chicken and white rice
- 3:45: arrive at the arena to stretch
- 4:15: shave head
- 4:30: walk onto the court and practice jump shots

Ray makes five shots from five different spots (both corners, both wings, and the top of the key), followed by five more shots from different distances (close to the rim, two steps back, midrange, college three-point range, and pro three-point range). In between those sets, he shoots five free throws. In total, he has to make 150 shots before he's done.

Ray never misses his pregame naps, and he doesn't take them because he's hungover — he doesn't drink. Nor does he skip his stretching every now and then. He follows his routine precisely *every* game. And here's the key — when he practices those jump shots, he does so at *game speed*. Here's what I mean. If you watch NBA players (or most ballplayers, for that matter) warm up, you'll notice they never move as quickly, or with as much purpose, as they do in games. Instead, they like to shoot the ball in a leisurely, unhurried manner.

But Ray understood early in his career that was foolish. What's the point of shooting a ball leisurely if that sort of motion is going to get your shot blocked in a real game? Instead, Ray takes every one of those practice shots at game speed. This means his body is bent low, his hands ready at his side as he catches the ball and springs into each shot. Just like he would in a real game.

The advantage Ray gains from this is obvious. While other players spend their warm-ups practicing shots they'll never be able to use in the actual game, Ray is training his body to take game shots almost instinctively. And it's not that other players don't know they'd be better off taking game shots in practice; it's just that they aren't disciplined enough to do it. Remember, it's exhausting to take 150 jump shots at game speed, especially when you've got an NBA game to play in a couple of hours. But Ray's body can handle it. He watches what he eats. And while he has a nice car, whenever Ray is home, he tries to bike as much as possible to build up his leg strength. It's a lifestyle that requires a ton of discipline, but Ray knows it's worth it.

So when Ray suddenly found himself with the ball with just seconds left at the end of Game 6 of the 2013 NBA Finals, with the Heat trailing by three, he didn't have to think about what to do. Instead, in one incredibly fluid motion, he used his well-conditioned legs to backpedal to the three-point line and then elevate for the three-pointer that tied the game.

It's been called one of the greatest shots in NBA history, one that secured Ray's reputation as one of the greatest players of his generation. But to say Ray made that shot because of his God-given ability or because he liked taking big shots is a cop-out.

No, Ray made that iconic shot because he had practiced it throughout his career — tens of thousands of times. So when it came time to take it, with millions of people watching and the Heat's season on the line, he didn't have to think about what to do. He simply implemented a skill he'd spent thousands of hours practicing and perfecting. That's the power of discipline.

My son, Dru, is another example of a player who tirelessly uses discipline as his personal rudder to excel at the game. As a short player in a big man's game, Dru had no choice but to rely on discipline to step up his skills. As a little kid, he had me shooting hoops with him in our driveway, and he refused to stop playing until he was able to beat me. Sometimes we'd be out there for six hours straight, late into the night, and I had to let him win just to get him to bed.

He was so devoted to his game that I remember him missing Super Bowl Sunday on more than one occasion simply because he refused to miss out on practicing. And remember, we lived in Ohio, which is rabid football country. Missing the Super Bowl simply wasn't something a young boy who was into sports would even consider in our neck of the woods. But Dru did so willingly, without complaint, in order to improve his game.

Nothing could trump his sense of intention when it came to showing up for his craft. From the moment he decided basketball was something he loved, he took it on himself to study it as if it were a research project for a master's degree. We're talking about a ten-year-old boy here, whose level of commitment was that sophisticated, that real.

So when Dru first met Bron, it was instant chemistry. They were like two peas in a pod, bound by their shared love of the game. Their ardor for basketball became the meeting place for their friendship, a platform on which they could regularly perform and deliver, each one inspiring and informing the other.

What drives your passion? When you're able to identify this crucial piece of the puzzle, you set yourself up to perform at a high level. Discipline is most authentically expressed when it comes with a genuine desire and pursuit.

IT'S A NUMBERS GAME

Earlier, I mentioned how Malcolm Gladwell's *Outliers* helped me get past the myth of the self-made man. But it is also a perfect reference for this chapter in which I hope to discredit another common misconception — the popular belief that success is a result of talent or luck. I'm not saying that extraordinary gifts are to be taken lightly or for granted. They are blessings and should be seen as such. But there is no getting around the fact that they are only one side of the coin.

Gladwell analyzed the key variables that relate to mastery and achievement and found one variable that connected many successful people: 10,000 hours. He found that 10,000 hours of practice (writing, painting, singing, playing an instrument, or participating in a sport — really anything one aims to master) spells the difference between those who succeed and those who linger on the periphery of their desire to do so. What does 10,000 hours look like? Well, consider this: if you practice two hours a day, it will take fourteen years to reach 10,000 hours.

"Practice isn't the thing you do once you're good. It's the thing you do that makes you good," he writes,* making the point that wanting something with your whole heart means absolutely nothing if you don't put in the hours to help bring it about.

Another book that sold me on the value of discipline is *Coach Wooden: One-on-One*. Coauthor Jay Carty poses the question, "If every morning your bank credited your account with $86,400 but every evening canceled whatever part of the amount you failed to use, what would you do?"† There are all kinds of answers — buy a new home, do a kitchen renovation, take a dream vacation. But the author explains that we have an account called time, and in this account we have 86,400 seconds in every day. So just as we can outline and justify how we would spend $86,400, we also need to be able to outline and justify how we're spending those 86,400 seconds each day.

I sometimes ask the guys I coach this question, just to get a sense of where their heads are. And of course, they can come up with plenty of things to do with $86,400 — buy a new car, a closetful of new sneakers, Xboxes, jewelry, you name it. They're never at a loss in coming up with things to spend that money on. But when I ask them how they'd spend the 86,400 seconds available to them each day, they're not as quick with their answers. "Remember, it's 86,400 seconds you can never take back," I always say. "How are you going to spend it? What are you going to do with it? Later on, will you regret how you spent all that precious time, or will you be proud, knowing you've made the best use of it?" The point I try to drive home is that if you use your time correctly, you are making an investment in your own legacy.

As a coach, I try to teach my players that time is the ultimate

---

* Malcolm Gladwell, *Outliers* (New York: Little, Brown, 2008), 42.

† John Wooden and Jay Carty, *Coach Wooden: One-on-One* (Ventura, CA: Regal, 2003), 20.

currency, not to be wasted and certainly not to be taken for granted. This is true not only for practice but for game time too. It's an especially important lesson for reserves who don't get much playing time. Let's be honest, there aren't a lot of players sitting on the bench who feel they belong there. Almost every reserve feels like they should be playing more than they do and are being wronged or overlooked by the coaches. As a result, it becomes easy for these players to pout when they're on the bench instead of staying focused on the game and cheering for their teammates who are playing. As a result, I've noticed that when I put a bench player in for a short stretch, they'll often take that sulking attitude with them on the court. Which, of course, is only going to make me even less likely to put them in a game for any meaningful stretch of time. It's the reason I always tell my bench players that if I put them in for only thirty seconds, they need to make those thirty seconds the best ones of their lives. Play your hardest for that period of time — no matter how brief you think it is. I don't care if we're up thirty points or down thirty points, play hard every second you're out there. Even if the game is already decided, the coaches are still watching to see who's going to make the most of their time. These kids need to understand that all we ever really have is the present moment.

While putting in the kind of hours Bron and Ray Allen dedicate to practice is certainly one of the keys to success, even that level of discipline alone often isn't enough. It's also crucial to develop the proper level of *motivation*. "Hard work is only a prison sentence when you lack motivation,"[*] Gladwell writes in *Outliers*, making the point that along with the willingness to commit, there has to be a wanting, a burning affinity to get there. It's as if desire is a candlewick that only gets lit and properly burns with the blaze of ongoing discipline. When it comes to mastery, it's not enough to simply practice. You have to *fall in love* with practicing; you have to make it your second skin. If you're not compelled by that which you have devoted yourself to, then maybe it's time to reevaluate your goals.

---

[*] Gladwell, *Outliers*, 108.

I'm a perfect example of someone who struggled with a lack of motivation. When I worked at ConAgra, I was caught in a routine that was the equivalent of the hamster-in-the-wheel scenario. I was working the grind daily and dutifully but never reaching a sense of personal satisfaction. Yes, I was disciplined in the sense that I went to work on time each morning, did my job to the best of my ability, and was truly grateful for the many blessings it gave to my family — but at the end of the day, I often asked myself, *What have I done that truly matters? What have I done that will have lasting impact?*

To make matters more complicated, I didn't fully believe in the products I was selling. For instance, one of the main items on my list was a sloppy joe mix. My job was to work with supermarket chains and convince their buyers to stock the sloppy joe mix. I would push the mix dutifully but not passionately, because I didn't use this product in my own life. Right after graduating from college, I stopped eating red meat and made sure my family didn't eat much of it either. I even had a period in my life where I didn't eat any meat except for fish. I don't think Dru had a hamburger until he was eleven or twelve years old. I didn't view red meat as being healthy for me or my family (though I have started eating it more often in recent years), so as you can imagine, I didn't make the best sloppy joe pitchman.

Even though I was aware that my lack of passion for corporate America had me spinning my wheels for several years, switching career gears at midlife can be a frightening prospect. Almost as soon as I started coaching, I could tell I was much more passionate about it than I was about selling processed foods to supermarkets, but would I be able to support my family doing it? I had no idea how to start. I knew I'd have to reinvent myself as a new kind of professional, which would require the discipline of a first-year student — except there were no teachers, no assignments, no curriculum, and no one to watch over my shoulder to make sure I did my homework. It was all on me. I needed to create an agenda of discipline that would teach me the basics of not only coaching but also event planning, which helped me to develop as a masterful coach and tournament director. And since I was a late bloomer, there would be no time to waste.

TRACING YOUR DREAM

It all really began when Dru showed an incredible zeal for basketball, and as his dad, I was compelled to help him walk down that path. He started playing at a local recreational league in Akron, where the guy who ran the league initially let him play on the condition that if he played, I'd have to be his coach. All the teams were in place, so to create my new team, they said I could have one player from each team. Of course, that one player was the weakest player — the one nobody wanted on their team. So you can imagine that my first attempts at coaching were less than ideal and, more to the point, provided for me a great exercise in patience and humility. We won one out of nine games, but still something told me I was doing the right thing.

Until that moment, I had been only a pickup basketball player, a weekend warrior kind of athlete who was more at home in a flag football game than anything else. After one season of coaching Dru's rec team, which I did on evenings and weekends, my job with ConAgra began demanding more of me, so I wasn't able to coach him the following season. However, I was still able to go to Dru's Saturday morning games, and one day, among the sea of African Americans, I noticed a lone white face in the stands, a gentleman who was furiously taking notes, which I found kind of odd. I couldn't imagine what was so urgent that he was scribbling with such gusto.

After the game, that very gentleman came over to Dru and me and said he liked the way Dru played and asked if he'd consider trying out for an AAU basketball team. Dru was delighted, of course, and so was I. He was in the fourth grade at the time, which caused the man to hesitate a bit because they were looking for fifth graders. But I pressed him to give Dru a try. It was one of those "significant moments" — one that catalyzed the shape of our lives.

Dru made the team, and though I wasn't surprised because I knew he had skill, I also knew it would be a whole new world of basketball for him — and for me. While the rec league was built around a sense of participation, the AAU league was more about competition. Because the stakes felt a little higher, I wanted to be around more to support my son, to have his back the whole way through. Growing up, I often saw dads help out with sports teams, so something about "father as supporter" made a lot of sense to me. For whatever reason, this culture of nurturing kept tugging at me.

When the fall season came around, the man who had been coaching the AAU team took a teaching position in a middle school and left the team. Some of the parents approached me to ask if I would consider taking the job. They had seen me help out in practice; I guess they just assumed I'd know what to do.

This was one of those moments, those divine cracks of light that blast open a person's world — a moment that gives a person no time to think and makes his heart race. I jumped on the opportunity because the truth is that I always wanted to be a coach. Somewhere deep inside me this dream had been buried, beneath layers of life, years, responsibility, and all those elements that somehow build on a person, so that by the time we reach a certain age, we often forget who we really are or what we really want.

Though I didn't know a lot about basketball as I started out, the one thing I did know with absolute certainty was that I was going to give it my all. I was committed to a standard of excellence, tapping into the cues I took from my pastor, who used excellence as a barometer for all of his life's actions. I already mentioned the mentorship I received from Bishop Johnson, but I need to emphasize the role of discipline or, better yet, the definition of discipline that I took from our pastor and applied to my life.

Until we began attending Bishop Johnson's church, my experiences with religion were not fulfilling. Besides the Sunday church services I went to with my family as a kid and my sister JoAnne's

Catholic Mass in New York (always spoken in Latin and, as such, feeling quite foreign to me), my only other experience with church came after I married Carolyn, who grew up in the Pentecostal tradition, which was also new to me. The services were long, filled with worship, and much different from the staid, traditional ceremony of my Methodist upbringing.

In 1984, I was promoted at work, and we moved from Pittsburgh to Akron. Carolyn and I began a search for a ministry where the word of God was taught with an emphasis on spiritual growth. From the moment I walked into The House of the Lord, the thing that impressed me most was the number of young black men at the service.

In our community, most of the church members tend to be women, but this church had a lot of men who weren't just sitting in the pews but were actively involved in the service. I was struck by the intentional engagement of the males in the sanctuary and excited by the sense of participation they shared with their wives and children. Their involvement was inspiring to me.

As we became more involved in the church, we saw that the church was run in a disciplined and ordered manner. Services started on time and ended at a reasonable time. Every detail of every service was organized and well planned. People were engaged in a number of different ministries — greeting, ushering, collecting offerings, making sure arrangements were made for baptisms and the Lord's Supper. All these teams had a leader who held regular meetings to make sure everything was done with excellence. Everything was conducted professionally and neatly as opposed to the haphazard way other places approached church life.

We were also impressed by the helpful ministries for young families — from a church school class for the newly married, which dealt with many issues that young couples face (finances, raising children, communication, and sex, to name just a few), to the Friday night teachers meeting, where Bishop Johnson spent time going deeper into Scripture.

SHAPING YOUR DREAM

This sturdy matrix of organization and accountability was new to us, and over the years it began to shape our own approach to navigating life. I've always felt that discipline is an attribute that isn't seen frequently enough in the African-American community, so it was incredibly motivating to be part of a community built around an ordered and structured approach. And don't forget, I'm talking about a community that began as a four-person congregation in our bishop's parents' living room. Its roots were extremely humble, but thanks to its disciplined approach, the church today has two-thousand-plus members and makes a profoundly positive impact on the community and its relationship with Jesus Christ.

Bishop Johnson never missed a Sunday back then. Being such a sought-after pastor, he had plenty of opportunities to speak elsewhere, which he steadfastly declined, which was a real testament to the commitment he held for his church. He didn't just talk the talk; he very much walked it.

Much of the success I've experienced after leaving corporate America and committing to a career in basketball can be attributed to the disciplined approach that Bishop Johnson taught me through his church. We'll talk more about this in a later chapter, but the words you never want to hear as an African American in a position of management are, "It was so disorganized." I have strived to never allow those words to be associated with anything I do, and the model set for me came from my pastor, Bishop Joey Johnson.

To become an excellent coach, I knew I had to show up to every practice with a plan. Even before practices began, I had to show my team that I held a vision — one that was grand enough and real enough for all of us to share. I had to show them that the road to making this dream come true was paved with milestones, and that together we could surmount even the toughest challenges out there.

And the more I invested in this uncharted territory, the greater my own love grew for the sport. As bored and listless as I had felt at my corporate job, as a coach I began to find joy in the everyday details. I started to cherish the little things, like the staccato sounds of sneaker sole squeaks against the wooden floor and the *thump-thump* of the balls being dribbled, like a fresh kind of heartbeat for my new day-to-day. I didn't even mind mopping the court, knowing that each cleaning was giving the boys a fresh slate on which to shine. The court became this utopian new office space where I could dig deep into the work that filled me the way nothing else had before.

Of course there were moments when I would become frustrated, when things did not, for whatever reason, go smoothly. It might have been a dispute with a kid (or, more likely, with one of their parents) over playing time, a disagreement with a player about strategy, frustration with a referee, or even the sense that I'd been outcoached. But part of the practice of discipline had to include the challenge of sticking it out, knowing that obstacles would always be par for the course and that quitting was under no circumstances an option.

It's important to remember that the road to actualizing one's dreams is often paved with less than perfect moments — moments that make you stop and ask, *Why on earth do I have to do this right now?*

We may not realize it at the time, but playing sports is one of the few times many people are able to shut out the noise of the world and simply focus on the task in front of them. Perhaps somewhat unexpectedly, the deeper I got into coaching basketball, the more I found myself growing spiritually. The last place I thought I would find myself fostering a closer connection to God was on a basketball court, but I suppose the act of serving these kids with life lessons and guidance became the meaning and depth I was longing for when I worked in sales for ConAgra. Teaching the boys and mentoring them became the central axis of my life around which everything else orbited. I wanted these kids to develop masterful basketball IQs, but it was even more important to me that they developed their own relationships with the Creator.

THE POWER OF GOING DEEP

If you accept the premise that discipline, not just desire, determines one's destiny, then you have to ask yourself, *What are the keys to becoming more disciplined?* My experience has taught me that prayer and meditation are two ways to do it. Through these "disciplines," for example, I have become more focused, which is a fundamental element in being able to shape a vision for a team.

The best days I ever have are the ones that begin with a moment of meditation. I'm not necessarily referring to the literal idea of meditation that's built into many Eastern teachings (though I'd bet that type of meditation is pretty close to or in keeping with what I'm about to describe), but really just a designated moment, ideally at the start of the day, to quiet the mind. Meditation means different things to different people, but for me it's really about finding that quiet place inside.

You know that inner voice inside your mind? The (almost neurotic) voice that first tells you how amazing you are and the next moment how terrible you are? The voice that tells you you're not good enough or you need to work harder or wants to know what's for dinner or if your friend is mad or if you have enough cash in your bank account to make the month's rent? That voice. That voice is always on, so our brains essentially become like giant rooms filled with a million television screens, each one flashing a different thought or emotion, all of them flashing at once at incredible speeds. It can get noisy and intense when we're trying to be the best versions of ourselves and navigate through our lives. Well, meditation is a way to gradually turn off those TV sets or at the very least turn down their volume so we can listen to the true whispers of our heart, our soul.

I don't have any prescribed way to do this, except for embracing the discipline to make sure I do it as often as possible — the goal being every day. I typically set aside about fifteen to thirty minutes in my office while sitting in a comfortable chair. I don't sit in a cross-legged advanced yoga position or anything like that. I'm not that guy. I just try to settle into some comfort and stillness. I try to have quality time to recognize what is inside of me rather than what is going on outside.

Usually I close my eyes and just follow my breath. I watch it move through my nostrils, observing its temperature and evaluating whether it's moving fast or slow, whether it's heavy or light, and whether it feels even or erratic. I just observe. After all, our breath is our force of life, the one thing that is a constant, no matter what is happening, as long as we're alive. This is why breath is such a great, basic, and universal tool for meditation. It's the one thing we all can use at any moment in our lives. Why do you think people always say to "take a deep breath" in a moment of crisis? Because conscious breathing is a great way to center and quiet the mind. And for me, that's what meditation is all about.

Sometimes I take it further and read a passage of Scripture or a piece of motivational or inspirational literature. Then I settle into my chair with my eyes closed and take in the essence of the words I've just read. Instead of speaking the words aloud or thinking about them too cerebrally, I allow *them* to speak to me. Instead of trying to rationalize or decipher them, when I'm in this quiet time of meditation, I just allow them to settle into me.

The main thing I try to accomplish through my prayer life is developing my relationship with my Lord and Savior. This quiet time allows Him to speak to me, whether through the words I read from Scripture or through the silence. I believe the heart is the center, not the mind, so I try to focus on the pleasant thoughts and feelings of the heart.

Like I said, this time of meditation and prayer always makes the day better, and it's a way of not giving in to the rat race we live in. Years ago, when I was a youth director at church, I heard a phrase that struck me: *the tyranny of the urgent.* I try to take those quiet moments to help me step away from the seemingly unstoppable urgency of everyday life.

And when I mute the voices that clamor for my attention, I am able to stay more focused on the principles I live by. The Scriptures speak about being "blown here and there by every wind of teaching" (Ephesians 4:14), which reminds me of the neurotic voice that keeps nagging at us. I am nowhere near silencing that voice for good, which is why the practice of daily meditation is so crucial.

Some people believe meditation is anti-Christian. Yet the question to ask yourself is, *What am I putting my mind to when I meditate?* If you're putting your mind to feeling love, you're in line with Christianity. This spiritual tool has helped me along the path to a stronger relationship with God. God has to speak to you through your own study. You don't have to always take someone else's word for how things should look. In our church, we talk about the idea that God is too big for us to put in a box that looks nice and neat. All I know is that this is how it is for me.

Those still moments give me the space to distill what's important in my life. In referring to everyday situations that cause us to have an emotional reaction, my pastor often asks, "Is this something I want to fall on the sword over?" What he means is, "Is this a life-or-death issue?" He brings this up a lot because he knows how prone we are to react to life's vicissitudes directly from our emotions. How we use our minds to *reason* things out is very important, but how we *react* to them is just as important. If you don't have a way to quiet those things, you're always going to be wound up. In Christianity we talk about salvation, but I believe salvation happens every single moment of every day. Can we save ourselves from our own reactions, which are based on emotions? Well, meditation is like a cool stream of water that naturally tames those emotional fires before they even start.

As a young kid, I heard the term *peace of mind*, and it really resonated with me. I suppose that's what I am really after. I find a lot of comfort in those peaceful moments — those quiet times of meditation that are there for me to understand that peace, to *feel* that peace.

It's not about understanding in a mental sense; it's more an inner revelation of how this peace should fill me and how it defines my relationship with God. My point is that even if you have a standard — and mine comes primarily from my Christian ethic — meditation is not a head knowledge but a heart knowledge. In those moments when emotions flare, how will you respond? Will you be the person who has a lot of wisdom but whose emotions won't allow them to do the right thing?

Centering is the key to everything I do. I try to set the tone by centering, maybe with a thought or with words, and I try to carry that sentiment throughout the day. I can't say it always works, but my odds for experiencing a great day are better when I start off this way. By the way, sitting in silence isn't the only way to go inward. Sometimes I get this sense of quiet and centering when I stretch. Just the act of moving and stretching my body helps me calm down and connect inside.

Can you think of a way to put meditative practice in your own daily routine? For some, it may be five minutes on the subway en route to work; for others, it can be that half hour of gardening work. Whatever it is, find it and commit to a daily practice of mental stillness, which will surely make more space for everything else in your life.

I've had many moments in my coaching career when I realized I was coaching from a place of anxiety. I was making decisions and calls based not on reason or the greater good of the team but instead on fear of failure, especially the dread of losing. But God puts signs in our paths, and I was fortunate to receive such a sign years ago when a friend gave me a quote from Scripture that declared an epic truth: "Do not be anxious about anything, but in every situation, by prayer and petition, with thanksgiving, present your requests to God" (Philippians 4:6). These words resonated deeply with me and armed me with the confidence of knowing that through prayer, I always have a line open with God. Now, whether we win or lose, I feel at peace, because in the end I truly believe we're going to figure it out, and even if we don't, life goes on.

The focus that prayer and meditation bring me not only aids in my shaping of a vision but also helps me teach the small details to my players that are the difference between being good and excellent.

Prayer and meditation have helped me be more accountable to my players because if I pray about us as a team becoming more unified and then I do or say something to the contrary, my players will call me out on it — which they should. In this way, prayer becomes a sounding board to constantly refer back to and a way to help them see prayer as the expression of collective goals.

Finally, and probably most importantly, prayer and meditation have disciplined me to stay in the present moment. Staying present allows me to correct, but not linger on, past mistakes and to not miss the importance of the journey by getting caught up in reaching a goal.

The practice of prayer and meditation is often challenging for people to master because of its seemingly intangible nature and because it means different things to different people. For some reason, we can get our heads around how important it is to exercise our bodies, but we tend to lose sight of how crucial it also is (perhaps even more) to work out our heart.

Part of my regimen of discipline as a coach includes starting every practice with a prayer or meditation. The act of playing basketball, or any sport, is so charged with the energy of competition that I find it is especially crucial among young athletes to tone down that heat and make space for deeper thinking. We pray before practices to remind ourselves that what we're doing is about more than just basketball, to forge a connection with the present in a way that means something beyond X's and O's.

Our prayers are about trying to better understand who God is and how He can use this moment, this practice, this time we're about to spend, to His glory and to our growth. I don't want prayer to be about winning or even about the thought of winning. Prayer is about us stepping back and honoring God in this present moment. If we want to see Him, we have to be present at every moment — the place where connection and growth truly occur.

Before our practices, I like to make sure the prayers are always different. I believe keeping this sense of dynamism lends itself to a more profound experience for the kids. Some days, the prayers are brief; other days, they are a bit longer; and sometimes they're about a certain event or a certain person. I don't want to use the same prayer every practice, because eventually they're going to stop listening to that message. I want each one to feel fresh and relevant to something that's happening in their lives.

I don't want them to resent these sacred moments by starting to feel they are part of some mindless routine or rote activity they are forced to trudge through. Instead, I want them to experience a jolt of inspiration, I want them to tap into a sense of gratitude, I want them to see and feel that basketball is really just one small slice of the pie.

These moments of introspection allow them to, even for an instant, forge a closer connection to their heavenly Father. Even though St. Vincent-St. Mary is a Catholic school, many of these kids don't consider themselves to be Christians or haven't yet developed their own spiritual practices. So I really try to treat these tiny windows into the consciousness as seedlings I'm planting toward their future links to God. Whether or not they are churchgoers or come from religious families, connection is connection, no matter how you slice it, and by designating time each day to these disciplines of prayer and meditation, we are able to see we are part of something greater than just ourselves.

We often see professional athletes thanking God in postgame media interviews. I have no problem with that. If someone wants to honor and thank God for giving them the athletic ability they have, it shows they understand that they're part of something bigger than themselves. It shows they know their talent and ability don't begin and end with themselves.

It's a good thing when someone honors or gives value to the success they've had. It should be a natural response, but it doesn't always have to look the same. Some athletes are more open or expressive, and others are more closed and personal. One is not better than the other. Just because I choose not to mention God when the TV cameras are on doesn't mean I don't have that connection. I just may want to show it in a more private way. I will say that at some level, we should be able to express these sentiments — whether in private or public, or just with those who are close to us. We need to be able to give God the honor and the glory.

My own spiritual journey has shown me again and again how necessary it is to carve out quiet time on a daily basis — a time to go inward and consciously reflect. We spend so much of our lives reacting to outside stimulation, taking life in, with our antenna forever up into the world. The concept of going inside is imperative because it gives us a framework in which to process all the circumstances that unfold in our lives. It gives us a sense of internal silence where we can listen more and react less, where we can try to tap into the whispers of our own soul's yearnings to figure out what needs to happen at any given moment.

Prayer and meditation give us a mirror into ourselves, which inevitably strengthens our connection to the Creator. People often perceive God as an angry, merciless ruler who is out to punish them. Part of my charge, my sacred responsibility, is to take the kids' understanding of God to another level. By sitting quietly in a world that seldom seems to stop, we can get a better, more accurate view of who we are and how we are meant to fit into the big picture. We can start to get a clearer sense of our unique purpose and teach ourselves how to take the steps to fulfill that purpose.

I like to think of it as an ongoing dance we have with the Creator, a harmonious movement between each one of us and God. He gives us opportunities to make choices in our lives, and it's our job to make the right ones in the most synchronized manner so we're not stepping on toes and messing up the healthy rhythm. The idea is that we are meant to move through it together, leading and following, following and leading — in this constant, grateful state of flow and grace.

We don't often recognize the self-control that's required in disciplining ourselves. That's why Scripture talks about striking a blow to our bodies and making them our slaves (1 Corinthians 9:27). We tend to lose sight of the fact that there's a spiritual battle going on inside each of us and that the question of who's going to win is always there for all. We forget all too often that giving in to the ego and to the desires of the flesh will always lead us down the path of destruction. And it can happen at any time of your life. It can happen to all of us. We can fall into some behavior that's not in our best interest if we don't fiercely cling to our sense of discipline.

Faith is believing everything depends on God and working like everything depends on *you*. Discipline is the *you* part. It is the missing link needed in whatever endeavor you take on in your life. Discipline is the fuel that allows you to stay committed to the task, no matter what life throws your way. Discipline is the work, the pointed focus that brings your desires into reality. And staying involved in the process without focusing on the results will keep you in the present moment, which fundamentally is the art of discipline.

CHAPTER 6

The Power of Words

Be impeccable with your word. Speak with integrity.
Say only what you mean. Avoid using the word to
speak against yourself or to gossip about others.
Use the power of your word in the direction of truth
and love.
Don Miguel Ruiz

I've always thought of myself as the quiet type, someone who tends to believe in the adage that "actions speak louder than words." But whether you're like me or more of a talker, none of us are exempt from seeking to gain a real understanding of the power of words.

I grew up with the idea that your word is your bond. Your actions need to line up with what you say, and when they do, people respect you more. That's what integrity is about. I'm the kind of person who believes that if I live what I say, people will watch me and take it in. And my model is Jesus Christ, who lived what He talked.

But since basketball is my vehicle, let's use a relevant analogy. What if we thought of each and every word that comes out of our mouth as if it was a crucial play in a high-pressure game, a move that has the power to dictate what will happen next?

Our words are packed with an energetic charge and can essentially make or break any situation — both for ourselves and for those at the receiving end of things. Words, despite being subtle and often thrown mindlessly into our everyday mix, are *always* loaded with possibility. As innocent as they may seem — mere configurations of letters in specific orders — our words are actually determiners of outcomes. They hold the power to be both malicious and medicinal. I firmly believe that every word spoken carries with it the potential for good or for bad.

I have witnessed again and again the ways in which carelessly spoken words of defeat or positive words of victory have affected the outcomes of situations. I mentioned in the last chapter that we pray before each game, not only to acknowledge God but also because I want my players to focus their thoughts on the task before them. Every word spoken, every supplication, every request, every one of the things we ask God to consider on our behalf, begins with a thought. If I can help them channel their thoughts in a positive direction, then I believe the words spoken on the court will be ones of victory. We create an energy of necessity by selecting a certain series of words in a particular order. We create intention with our words. On the flip side, some of our moments of defeat have been those times when collectively the team has focused on all the negative aspects of the game.

But let's take it even further back. The Bible describes how God created the world through nine statements ("And [or "Then"] God said"; Genesis 1:3, 6, 9, 11, 14, 20, 24, 26, 29), that He willed creation into being just by *saying so*. Think about that for a minute.

Then in Ephesians 4:29, the apostle Paul wrote, "Do not let any unwholesome talk come out of your mouths, but only what is helpful for building others up according to their needs, that it may benefit those who listen." And Proverbs 16:24 reads, "Gracious words are a honeycomb, sweet to the soul and healing to the bones." There are many other examples throughout the Bible where the use of words is mentioned and elaborately scrutinized. Whether or not you believe or ascribe to these teachings, it's hard to ignore how often and how seriously words are taken in these writings.

I began this book with a detailed description of our defeat at the state championship game against Roger Bacon High School during my first year as head coach. It was downright painful. Not only because it cost us a championship but also because of everything that led up to the loss, along with the immediate aftermath, a lot of which has to do with the power of words.

To understand the atmosphere, remember that before we played the state championship game during Bron's junior year, the combination of fame (fueled by the media that followed every move Bron made) and arrogance (the result of the boys getting overly confident) had created an attitude of nonchalance that was new to our group.

Of course, I was not free from blame. Like I said before, being the coach of such a successful team with the kind of momentum they were revving up inevitably changed my approach. I became fixated on winning a championship and started losing sight of the principles that had drawn me to coaching in the first place. And even though I was frustrated about the boys' cockiness and the media hullabaloo that began to surround us, controlling any of it felt beyond my grasp. I suppose I surrendered to a certain degree, though I was in denial about my shortcoming until the final buzzer sounded.

When the season was over, it was devastating for so many reasons, not the least of which was the fact that Dru's failure to keep his emotions in check had factored into our loss.

As I already wrote, Dru's inexplicable technical foul in the game's final nine seconds essentially sealed the victory for Roger Bacon. When the game was over, my team was in shambles. Willie, who had barely gotten off the bench during the game, was in tears. Romeo went completely dark, his eyes wild with rage, and he looked like he was ready to hit the first person to cross his path. Dru was sobbing inconsolably, while Sian, who refused to wear the second-place silver medallion in protest, tried in vain to calm him down. I later found out

Romeo's rage went as far as flushing said medallion down the toilet of the locker room, his own attempt at erasing the reality that had just unfolded. Bron didn't cry. While he was frustrated with Dru III for getting that unnecessary technical foul, he, more than the others, seemed to accept the defeat. He walked over to the Roger Bacon players and shook their hands, his expression earnest but his heart broken.

Despite Bron's stoicism, the boys' pain was palpable, as was mine. I didn't sleep that night following the game, rehashing its twists and turns, wondering what I could have done differently, and feeling particularly vexed about what I felt were the refs' tighter-than-usual calls.

But the real torment kicked in when I woke up the next morning and opened the morning papers. One headline in particular seemed to broadcast my deepest insecurities to the entire world, blaring out, "When the team needed him most, Coach Dru Joyce let them down."

When I saw those words for the first time, I felt the anger bubbling up inside me like an ulcer, burning me on the inside, demanding that I react. This writer didn't know anything about me or what I had done. I was just a pawn to throw around for dramatic effect in his own theater of journalistic censure. Never mind that they discounted every iota of intention I had genuinely implemented for the sake of the boys since 1995.

I felt my defenses kicking in like a boxer's fury. I was ready to pounce. I wanted that writer to know every little thing I had ever done for those boys. Forget about whether or not we had won a basketball game; I needed him to know I was not only their coach but also their mentor, their guide, and their number one fan. I felt desperate for him to understand just how much of my time and energy I had given them over the course of the years. I needed him to get the fact that my whole purpose in life during that moment in my career (and as a father to one of the players!) was to *never* let them down.

That piece of scrutiny (which was just one of many scathing lines that ran in the papers that day) tore through me like claws. I was crushed, carrying not only the pain of a tarnished state championship legacy the boys were desperate to hold, but even more so, the smearing words of the journalists, who seemed to be having some kind of perverse and celebratory field day with this particular defeat.

But just as words can hurt, they can also heal.

After reading the articles, I sat in a slump of my own grief at our kitchen counter with the grim array of local sports sections fanned out in front of me like a collage of bad news. My head hung low and was spinning with doubt and regret, and I was bleary-eyed from lack of sleep. I didn't know how to face the day, much less myself. I literally felt broken.

I heard my son's footsteps, and my first instinct was to shake my head, still unable to come to terms with having to face anyone, much less Dru, whose eyes I was afraid to meet. I was not prepared to have that talk. I had no words for him.

Luckily, I didn't have to.

In that moment, it was *his* words that saved me. He came over cautiously, looking at the strewn-out newspapers, neither of us having to say anything about the headlines to take in how they hurt. "Don't worry about it, Dad. We're going to show them next season," he said, each word cool and calming like a drop of liquid aloe on a nasty, bloody cut.

But the pain was still too raw, and so was I. "I'm going to write this reporter a letter," I said, feeling the bitterness inside me. "Who does he think he is?" I was angry, but at the core of my anger was hurt. I had taken responsibility for the fact that we didn't win, but to have this writer, who didn't know me, lash out at me with this critique was not something you want to wake up to the day after. It killed me to know my son had to bear witness to the whole debacle, that we were a part of it together.

"Dad, leave it. Don't waste your time writing that guy a single word. Let's just show him instead," my wise young son said with his trademark determination. I looked up for the first time in what felt like hours and noticed my wife was now standing in the kitchen too — the three of us bound by this moment of difficulty and togetherness. I suddenly felt warm and safe again, remembering in that instant what really matters.

Then Carolyn chimed in. "Dru's right," she said and came over to me, her physical presence like a warm, cozy light shining on the bleakest of moments. "Besides, journalists love to feed off other people's hardships. That's their problem. Let's go out there and show everyone who we really are," she said, warming my soul with her potent, healing words. In that instant, I remembered the words of Proverbs 12:18: "The words of the reckless pierce like swords, but the tongue of the wise brings healing."

The biting words of the media slashed into me that awful morning, and my family's words served to sew me back up. And it hit me that "what goes up must come down," but the opposite is also true; and with the support and encouragement that came up that day in the form of my loved ones' loving words, I was ready to climb again.

REAL TALK

I read recently a book that deserves mention here. By now you probably know how I feel about books and the profound, life-changing impact they can have on any mind, young or old. I always tell my kids that *readers are leaders*, and in light of what we're talking about here — the power of words — let's for a moment acknowledge the fact that the potentially powerful ideas within books come into our consciousness through the printed word.

The book I read is *The Four Agreements: A Practical Guide to Personal Freedom* by Don Miguel Ruiz. In it, Ruiz shares inspiring insights on how to live with authenticity and also sheds light on how we can effectively use and perceive words. His book is an easy read, a compact book that packs enough punch to evoke real change, mostly because the lessons it espouses are universal and real.

Ruiz's first agreement tells us to be impeccable with our word — to practice cultivating a keen sense of awareness when it comes to every single word, every sentence that leaves our lips. Being impeccable with our word also means we hold an ongoing commitment to speak the truth, with the deep understanding that our words are like energetic ricochets that can dent and scar if poorly fired off. If our words pack such punch, we should make sure their impact is full of positivity, that they serve to lift and not lessen.

I'll give you an example of a time when I wasn't impeccable in my speech and underestimated the value of my words and the negative impact they had on someone I love. Sadly, the recipient of those words was my daughter, Ursula, and though my intentions were, of course, never malicious, the words left a mark on her that I wish I could take back.

My daughter, being in the throes of all the various things young girls face growing up, sometimes reacted to situations with what I felt was a bit of extra emotion. In response to some of Ursula's unpredictable bouts of sentiment, my wife and I would sometimes jokingly refer to her as a "drama queen." We meant no harm, and the last thing we wanted to do was add fuel to the ever-burning fires of preteen angst, but that's exactly what we did.

Thankfully, we have a close-knit, communicative family, because my wife and I found out about Ursula's hurt feelings through our other daughter, India, with whom Ursula regularly shared her feelings about growing up. Apparently, our habit of calling her a drama queen was painful to her and made her feel we didn't take her seriously. The feeling lingered even into adulthood, which is when she vented about it with her sister.

Our daughter has grown up to be a wonderful young woman, and I like to believe she has forgiven us for our shortsightedness when we called her a "drama queen" back in the day. But I'd be lying if I said such quips didn't hurt her and put a dent in her self-esteem.

These comments, as "meaningless" as they seemed to us,

became etched in our daughter's life script, which could have been avoided if Carolyn and I had been more attuned to being impeccable with our speech. After our conversation with India, I called Ursula and apologized for how our words had affected her, even into adulthood. I made it clear our intentions were never to make her feel like we didn't care, and I confessed we had been insensitive to the challenges she had been going through. The conversation and my apology healed our relationship in an area where I never knew healing was required — and it centered around the power of words.

Even though I felt bad about hurting my daughter's feelings, I came away feeling proud of my girls for talking about it and confiding in each other. I think much of what plagues kids today is the result of them just not talking to each other and communicating. They're so busy trying to put on a tough exterior that they forget how basic and important the act of expressing actually is. And so I always try to tell the kids I coach to look to one another as sounding boards, to initiate conversations about whatever happens to be on their mind.

Not only do we have to understand that our own words carry a punch, but we also have to be careful not to give the words of other people undue power over us. I, too, missed this lesson when I allowed the severe words of the media to consume me the morning after the state championship game. People will always have some kind of personal agenda in their behavior and speech. Instead of seeing the media's critique of me as someone's opinion or a reflection of someone's own agenda, I chose to internalize their comments and, for a moment (even if it was short-lived), allowed myself to be defined by those individuals' views. They may have been wrong to hurl such views so nastily, but I was even more wrong to let them settle in and bring misery to my spirit.

Instead of identifying with the painful words that come our way, we should see them for what they are — someone else's point of view. The lesson here is to file such attacks under "Things I Can't Control," and rather than letting them seep into us, we should watch them dissipate into thin air.

It's also important to be clear and concise with our words so people are less likely to make assumptions. In my business and personal relationships, I've seen the damaging impact of making assumptions, so I go out of my way to make sure my players are clear about my expectations for them. When they make the team, I share with them the significance of being a part of the St. Vincent-St. Mary tradition. I hold a preseason meeting for the parents in which I stress my expectations of them. I don't want them to assume I have an open-door policy that allows them to come and vent their frustrations about playing time, strategy, or other players. I make it clear I will only talk with them about their son and his development. The antidote to making assumptions is to request clarity, to seek truth, to use one's words to demystify that which we're not sure of, especially when it comes to communicating with people we love, work with, or come into contact with in our sphere of influence.

I remember reading about a Christian coach in a Division II school in Oregon who had seven principles — words, really — that our team ended up adopting: unity, discipline, thankfulness, servanthood, passion, integrity, and humility. We posted these words on the wall of our locker room as the last thing the boys would see before they made their way onto the court. We made this simple gesture to embrace the fact that words can have a wonderfully positive influence. We can speak our reality into existence, which is why it's crucial to focus on positive words and thoughts. As Jesus put it, "By your words you will be acquitted, and by your words you will be condemned" (Matthew 12:37).

CHAPTER 7

The Heart of
a Servant

Life's most persistent and urgent question is: what are you doing for others?   *Dr. Martin Luther King Jr.*

It may sound odd, but much of what I loved about playing on the youth football team when I was in elementary school had absolutely nothing to do with football. I mean, sure, I loved the game itself — the running, the thrill of trying to juke a would-be tackler, the sound of the mashing of pads, and the sense of exhausted satisfaction when the game was over. But looking back on those days, one of the main things that drew me in was the sense of *service* that made each and every one of our games possible.

Right along with the kids running around in grass-stained uniforms and full of competitive spirit, adrenaline, and burgeoning talents stood the parents. There on the sidelines were the many moms and dads who volunteered for our benefit, who made it a point to give of their time so their kids, *we* kids, could play the game of football to our heart's content. So we could *have* something. So we could *be* something.

The fathers drove kids to and from practices and games and served as coaches, motivating and guiding us through each moment of each game. The mothers dutifully worked the concession stands, serving up cold sodas and tasty snacks to the fans on the sidelines, creating an atmosphere of loving recreation where we all felt at home. Everyone behaved as though these games meant everything, as if nothing outside of that particular afternoon mattered as much as those moments did, to the point where I almost assumed they were being paid to do these jobs. Well, they weren't.

Knowing what I now know, those adults had undoubtedly been very busy, with plenty of things they could have been doing with their time. Forget about just a little bit of weekend R&R — there was work to be done around the house and errands to run, to say nothing of catching an extra weekend shift at the steel mill or pottery to bring in desperately needed cash. And yet there they were, serving the kids, sacrificing their own personal time for the sake of the younger generation. I'm sure part of why they did it was to take a load off and have a little fun supporting their children, but I know they were also there because football kept us off the streets and out of trouble. And they also knew — more than we realized — that those weekend days running up and down a dusty field were some of the best times we were ever going to have in East Liverpool. They knew the kinds of struggles that awaited us not far down the road, and they wanted us to enjoy life to the fullest while we still could. They gave of themselves for our benefit.

Perhaps I took special notice of these parents because my own were seldom there. As I mentioned earlier, my mother was a day worker and my father was a janitor. They had to work hard — sometimes seven days a week — just so we could eat. And we didn't own a car either. But observing the presence of other parents — those who had a little more leisure time on their hands but who gave that time to us — helped shape my appreciation for the idea of self-sacrifice that I believe is at the core of what it means to have the heart of a servant. Two words come to mind when I think about a servant's heart: one is *service*, and the other is *selflessness* — and the two go hand in hand.

From the instant we leave our mothers' wombs, our needs are

somehow magically met. If we cry, we get a bottle; if we soil our diapers, someone changes them; even if we have to burp, someone is miraculously there to make sure we get every last drop of air out of our little tummies. These are nature's guidelines, of course, because newborn babies certainly can't take care of themselves. The problem is that as we grow up, we cling to these guidelines. We get used to other people doing things for us, used to wanting someone else to do the dirty work, and (metaphorically) crying when something doesn't go our way.

Growing up doesn't just mean getting bigger or getting older. It means coming out of the delusion that we are here just for ourselves, just to have our own needs met. It means realizing we were put on this earth to make a difference. It means stepping further and further away from the misconception that we *deserve* things and more into the idea that we are here to *serve*.

As I move through life, I'm always looking for ways I can serve and give back to my community. After all, the primary reason I was drawn to coaching was that it provided me with an opportunity to serve others. I can't think of a greater job than one that allows me to positively impact young people's lives on a daily basis, one that makes me truly proud to be a servant.

Pause for a moment to reflect on some of the ways you can give back. It's OK to get creative about this, as giving back doesn't necessarily have to happen monetarily. Sometimes a phone call to someone in need, a handwritten note expressing gratitude, or even a pat on the back of someone who accomplished something substantial can go a long way.

SERVE BEFORE DESERVE

When people step away from the habit of "taking" and enter the space of "giving," I believe they become not only more fulfilled but healthier spiritually. Giving back is like a statement to the heavenly

Father that says, *Thank you for what you've given me*. It's like a nod of gratitude combined with a battery pack that energizes possibility for someone else.

I'll give an example. We always had events and activities going on as part of our church's youth ministry, of which I was the director. One of the things I fondly remember doing was volunteering with the kids on a Habitat for Humanity project.

This amazing Christian housing ministry, founded by Millard and Linda Fuller in 1976 under the guiding principle that every man, woman, and child should have a decent, safe, and affordable place to live, gave us a chance to build homes from the ground up for families in need.

I recall one of the first times we reported for duty as a group to begin our work at one of the homes. We showed up at our designated site at the crack of dawn, not quite knowing what to expect, all of us humbled by the vacant expanse before us where this home was to be erected. Just the act of gazing on this massive emptiness gave us such perspective, showing us the physical reality of what it means to *have* a home at all. It made us instantly grateful for our own dwelling places, hitting each of us with the reality of how much we take for granted on a daily basis, when many folks don't even have four walls and a roof to call their own.

At first we all looked at each other, wondering how this would all play out. We didn't know anything about carpentry, much less about the elaborate engineering elements that go into constructing a home. We almost couldn't believe the task we had taken on, but there we were, united in the fact that we had, for better or worse, agreed to do this.

But of course, the Habitat program had been around long enough that its managers knew exactly what they were doing. There was an organized, preplanned protocol in place, which made it possible for anyone to walk onto a site and do a job. We were separated into groups, and each one received a set of instructions, along with the tools and hardware necessary to accomplish our tasks. We got hammers, nails, screwdrivers, wood, levels, and saws — all kinds of equipment we needed to do the work. Team leaders helped manage each task, and slowly but surely, we were on the way to creating something together.

The look on the kids' faces meant everything to me, as I saw them tap into the understanding that they were actively giving their time, their energy, for something that had absolutely nothing to do with their own wants or needs. In those moments they got a real taste of sacrifice. I'm sure many of the kids (and I too) would have preferred spending that Saturday at the gym playing hoops or running around a football field or goofing off at Perkins Pool. But we used our time that day to serve Habitat and the people who would one day live in the home we helped build. And not only was our service inherently a positive thing, but it also felt incredibly good, despite the hot sun and hard work.

This attitude of service wasn't shared only with the kids at church. As a coach, it was always crucial to me that my players understood the value of having the heart of a servant. I needed them to see the merits of self-sacrifice, not just because it would help them become better players but more so because it would compel them to become great individuals.

During the holiday season, a local church created food baskets for needy families. It may not sound like a major feat, but the labor that went into making these baskets and getting them to the right places was beyond tedious and took a lot of time and energy. *Time and energy* — these are the building blocks of servanthood.

The boys and I helped unload tractor-trailers full of fifty-pound bags of potatoes and cases of canned goods. We carried them to the church basement, where volunteers sorted them. Do you think a bunch of teenage boys wanted to do this type of labor? We all know the answer. Sure, I'd hear the occasional grumble or wisecrack, but I knew that at the end of the day, they were glad they had helped out.

These moments injected them with a sense of empathy for the needy families that would benefit from their diligence, and it also gave them quality time to bond as a group off the court, when they could tap into other aspects of life that were just as important, if not more so, than their own basketball-related desires and goals.

Sometimes we got together to serve meals at local homeless shelters, which was always eye-opening and humbling, even for the kids who weren't in the best situations themselves. During those moments I couldn't help but think of my own parents, who occasionally worked as servers at a country club for the rich just to make ends meet. And here we were, serving food to the poor. It helped show me the struggles of life are relative, and in one way or another, we are all always helping one another. Or at least we should be.

Just as I encouraged the players to give as much and as often as they could, my wife and I also did our best to help the boys on the team if they needed anything. Whether it was clothes or books for school or money to put on their ID cards for lunch — whatever it was, giving back gave us a sense of purpose beyond our roles as parents and husband and wife. It cemented the commitment we pledged to them — me as their coach and Carolyn as my noble accomplice.

After all, how many road trips and caravans did my wife copilot, helping me transport a slew of sweaty, excited boys and their gear to this or that tournament? How many games did she videotape for us so we could analyze the team's performance afterward? And how many weekends did she give up her own time to cook for and look after the boys who camped out at our house? For all my years of service as coach and mentor, Carolyn was also making tremendous sacrifices so these boys could live out their dreams.

I always tried to help my family and my players see that by

sharing these blessings with others, they were actually creating more blessings for themselves. I'm proud to say both of my daughters embrace this message in their own lives, as they are involved in professions of service. My oldest, Ursula, has worked for several nonprofit organizations that serve people seeking to get their lives together and people who have suffered head trauma. She's currently starting her own consulting company to help service organizations meet government standards and earn grant money. India started her own nonprofit called STARS (Sisters Transforming and Reaching Success), which helps teenage girls through the trying times of adolescence. And now my youngest son, Cameron, is beginning his own journey into coaching.

At the end of the day, it isn't so much about what you do but more about the fact that you're doing *something* to help others. It's the intention, the conscious allotment of time and energy to something that may not be the exact thing you feel like giving it to at that moment.

When I first started participating in these types of service, I wasn't always sure I understood the significance. But then I'd come across a player who would return, a little older, looking for a way to help, to give back. I can think of at least twenty guys right now who have at some point come back and found a way to give back.

And truthfully, this commitment to service is at the heart of Bron's "return" to Cleveland, which took place just as I was finishing this book.

Now the reason I put quotes around "return" is that, as anyone who lives in Akron can tell you, Bron never really left. Yes, he went to the Heat for four years, but he remained a part of Northeast Ohio, both emotionally and physically. His LeBron James Family Foundation continued to create opportunities and provide support for children in the area, and he remained a constant — and beloved — presence around Northeast Ohio in the off-season.

After Bron opted out of his contract with the Miami Heat, a lot of folks assumed I had inside information about his next move.

But honestly, I didn't know. I did, however, suspect he might come back to the Cavs because I knew just how much this area means to him. I knew that giving back to his community would weigh into his decision just as much, if not more, as what was best for him in his basketball career.

This is what Bron alluded to when he wrote in *Sports Illustrated* that his presence can make a real difference in Northeast Ohio.[*] Forget about the money his return to the Cavs will bring to the area, or even the civic pride the community will feel when the team eventually wins a championship, which I believe in time it will.

Instead, what Bron is alluding to is this idea of giving back, of serving one's community through one's time, energy, and effort.

THE PROBLEM WITH SELFISHNESS

But there's always a flip side. I've come to understand that the opposite of service and selflessness is *entitlement*, which, if not tamed, can get a person — or a group of people — in a lot of trouble.

One of my goals as a coach is to teach selfless basketball, team basketball. I firmly believe it's about the team and not just an individual player. When Bron started playing on the Shooting Stars Travel Team (AAU), he was like most young kids — he shot the ball most of the time. But I could see he had the vision and ability to make plays. I remember driving him home from practice one evening, and I told him that if he shared the basketball, teammates would always enjoy playing with him. I never had to have that conversation with him again. He got it. When your best player creates opportunities for other players, it becomes contagious. As Bron grew, so did his excitement about creating shots for other players. I also raised both of my sons as traditional pass-first point guards. This selfless style of play has been emphasized with every team I've ever coached.

---

[*] LeBron James, as told to Lee Jenkins, "I'm Coming Home," July 11, 2014, www.si.com/nba/2014/07/11/lebron-james-cleveland-cavaliers (accessed October 18, 2014).

It hasn't always been easy to implement, especially since many of today's young players have been trained to think "me first," and by the time they reach high school, this attitude has been deeply ingrained into their consciousness. I believe God has gifted me with the talent to bring individuals together to work toward a common goal. Each year, it has become more challenging to achieve this unity because of the attitude of entitlement — the mind-set that says, "It's all about me." I stress to my players that if they are willing to sacrifice for the team, they can achieve their individual goals. However, getting them to believe this requires some convincing on my part.

My most difficult team in the area of selfishness occurred in the 2010 – 2011 season. The school year started with our best player transferring, which left a void at the top. He wasn't the team leader, but everyone on the team liked him. With him gone, each player believed he was the one to save the team. A "me first" attitude developed, and the core players had grown up as rivals, so they really didn't like each other. This led to a team filled with opposition (from the parents all the way down to the players), selfishness, resentment, anger, jealousy, and you name it — I think every possible negative attitude was there.

I finally recognized it all stemmed from two players who couldn't get along. I brought them into my office and told them I believed they were the problem, and if they didn't get their relationship fixed, the team would keep struggling. It was their senior season, and I challenged them to put aside their petty differences and play to win their last game. I can't say they became best friends, but they mended their relationship enough to make it work for the group, and we went on to win our third state championship.

USE YOUR SKILL FOR THE GREATER GOOD

Sometimes being a servant means knowing how to identify one's individual talents and using the specific skill set to contribute for the greater good.

This reminds me of a young man from my 2009 team, Mike Hammonds. Because he had evolved into a great player, all the other kids greatly respected him. He had come to us unheralded, but with time and hard work, he just kept getting better. He'd patiently wait his turn on the bench, give it his all when he was on the court, and never complain.

By the time his senior year came along, he had stepped up and become one of the best players on the team. There were a lot of times, though, when he'd be messing around when the occasion called for seriousness. Because of his skill and work ethic, I wanted him to be the leader of the team. Daylen Harrison was our best player, but Daylen was quiet, a hard worker who led by example but not the vocal leader the group needed.

From my experience, I knew kids need leaders who are a bit more vocal and charismatic, so I gently pushed Mike to get out of his shell and grow up a bit, knowing it would be good for both him and the team.

But every time I pushed, he resisted. It became clear he didn't want the burden of responsibility; he was more interested in having fun.

"All the other kids are following you," I said one afternoon. "Your behavior and attitude have the power to take this team in either the right or the wrong direction. You're going to play a big role in determining whether we have a lot of guys out there messing around or a lot of guys focused on making this team better. " I realize it may have been a heavy load to drop on him, but I sincerely believed he was up to the challenge.

But he still resisted, so I had to get a little tougher with him. If he'd act up a little bit during a workout, instead of letting it slide, I'd send him to the showers. One time his mother was at a preseason open gym, and he went off on a young freshman for no real reason, probably just to get a laugh. It was uncomfortable, but I threw him out, with his mother watching.

"Mike, you gotta go," I said in a matter-of-fact tone. I needed to show him that anything short of being a leader was unacceptable. After the open gym, he came into my office with his mother. We talked at length about how he had treated the freshman player and how much the players looked up to him. I remember going home that night excited to tell Carolyn I had found my leader. Or so I thought.

There are two things my players know you don't do to Coach Dru: you don't wave me off, and when you're walking off the court, you don't pull out your jersey.

The early season practices were great. Daylen was playing well, and Mike was playing exceptionally well. Then the wheels fell off. We were participating in a twelve-team scrimmage in Toledo. Mike got off to a rough start. Not only did he turn the ball over twice, but he also fouled a jump shooter, which is another no-no. I sent in a sub so he could calm down a little bit. I started to say something as he left the floor, but he waved me off. As he sailed past me to sit down, he started to pull out his jersey. I grabbed his wrist as if to say, *Mike, don't go there*. His response was, "Get your f***ing hands off me." At that point, I calmly told him he was done — not just for the day but also for the season. As I said earlier, it was a twelve-team scrimmage, which meant we'd usually play four teams. All this happened during our second game, so Mike sulked in the school cafeteria for the rest of the day.

His mother called during a break between our third and fourth game and pleaded with me on her son's behalf for a second chance, but I told her the truth. "Look, none of my players are going to come at me like that and stay on the team."

When I got home that evening and told my wife what had happened, she gave me a look and said, "Why are you throwing Mike off the team?"

The expression on my face said it all — *I just wasn't going to have that kind of behavior on my team*.

"That's the easy way out," Carolyn said. "A month ago you were all excited 'cause you had found your leader, and you were going to groom him. Now you're done with him? Are *you* going to step up or take the easy way out? *You* need to lead by example." She had made her point.

So the next day, I called Mike into the office.

"You're not going to win this battle, Mike. You're going to come back and apologize to the team. And not only are you going to apologize, but you're going to lead this team in the right direction," I said, presenting him again with the opportunity to serve. "If you don't, I'm still going to win because if I throw you off again, you won't be back, and everyone else will fall in line because they'll say, 'If he threw Mike off and he's been playing great, he will surely throw me off.'"

We looked each other dead in the eyes, and I could tell he was finally ready to accept this sacred duty. I could see he understood what real leadership entailed, and that by being a leader, a person takes on a very special kind of accountability, one that can make or break the group. He started to see that a leader has the power to color the whole tone and character of a team, and that leading with positivity can yield amazing results.

He knew I didn't come after every kid like this, that I had singled him out because I saw real potential in him and this was a moment that could not only set him apart but also help shape his path.

He accepted my challenge, and after he apologized to the team and to me, he stepped back in with sheer determination to keep playing the best ball *and* to become the leader we all knew he could be. Whenever there was an issue, he became my go-to guy. If the younger guys needed a pep talk, Mike would amp them up. If someone was arguing, Mike would break it up. He himself started to see the value of having a player lead the team. And I started to see him as my right-hand man, who delivered dutifully, with the heart of a servant.

One day in the middle of January, he came into my office and said, "Coach, we're going to win the state championship." And when he said that, I knew we would. And we did, not only because Mike played terrific basketball but also because he helped shape the direction of the team.

It's one thing to have a great coach guiding and mentoring a team; it's an entirely different story when there's a natural-born leader on the team, one of the players themselves who can command respect and serve as the compass for the group. Such a leader gives the team a sense of built-in power, a feeling that it is not only held together but also focused in its mission.

BE SELFLESS IN YOUR SERVICE

One of my favorite John Wooden expressions is this: "It's amazing how much can be accomplished when no one cares who gets the credit." This idea, too, belongs in the discussion of what it means to have the heart of a servant, because when someone is overly concerned with getting the credit or receiving the glory, it's usually a strong indication that they're only really there to serve *themselves*.

Players do this for all kinds of reasons — recognition, popularity, and competitiveness, to name just a few. A lot of seniors will play hard just to get scholarships. But the truth is that if you win a state championship *as a team*, you'll ultimately get everything you want as an individual and more. This is why it's crucial to always put the team first. When you prioritize the team, you are in service; when you prioritize yourself, the only thing you serve is your ego.

This is a particularly challenging insight to instill in young kids who are jacked up with so much enthusiasm for the game and are dying to get out there and play. But once they do get it, and many of them eventually do, they start seeing the big picture of the team and its needs and gradually learn that part of what it means to have the heart of a servant is to demonstrate *patience*.

One of the greatest obstacles I face as a coach is getting kids to understand they might have to wait their turn, that they might not play varsity until their sophomore or even junior year. Again, not every player can be a Bron or a Dru III and play varsity for four years. I try to give them a silver lining by explaining that by then they'll be further along because of the system and what we're teaching, and that they'll also get to perform on a bigger stage. But in our culture of instant gratification, it's hard to make that point to the eager kids (and often to their even more eager parents).

In those instances I say, "Listen, success as a basketball player wasn't promised to you. You need to work hard and struggle. And if you love it and want it that much, you need to sacrifice your time and energy, and more than anything, you need to be patient."

And when they inevitably want to compare themselves to other kids who get more playing time than they do, I level with them and say, "It's not that you're not good enough — but you're not *better than*. And if you're not better than the guy in front of you, you're going to have to be patient. And if you can show me you're willing to wait your turn for the good of the team, chances are I'll increase your minutes."

Service is about patience and sacrifice, but it's also about *attitude*. If you come in with the right attitude and work hard during practice, you will get my attention. You'll be lighting a fire under me to find ways to sneak you into games.

Another hint for anyone who finds themselves stuck on their team's bench: When you're on the bench, remember that it's not all about you. Cheer for your team, even if you are consumed with a desire to be in the game. Guess what? You can be of service to your team right from the bench. The guys on the court feel the energy that comes from the fans, so you better believe they're going to feel it when it's coming from their own brothers on the bench.

On the other hand, if your head is down and you're sulking, that energy will radiate to everyone — to the guys on the court and certainly to me. I'll be turned off, and I'll just look for someone else to put in. Frankly, if you go into the game like some kind of victim, as a coach I very quickly lose interest.

As I said at the beginning of the chapter, service equals selflessness, and once you're off the bench, I'm still always looking for selfless players. And one of the best ways to assert your selflessness is to take a charge. That means if one of your teammates gets beat and his man is heading for an easy score, slide over and put your body between him and the basket. By sacrificing your body for your teammate's mistake, you're not only potentially saving the team two points, but you're also virtually guaranteeing that I'll take note of your selflessness.

Why am I going to notice? Because on a basic level, I know very few people like to get run over by a player who's driving to the basket. But when you give up your body like that, I know you're serious about the team. And since no one records stats for charges taken, at least not at the high school level, I know you're not doing it to pad your stat sheet. I know your friends on the team or up in the stands don't put value on that sort of play. There's very little ego in taking a charge but plenty of selflessness, which I love to see as a coach.

In his comment about getting credit, Coach Wooden talks about something these boys had to contend with quite a bit. You can imagine what it must have been like to play on the team that brought LeBron James into the public eye. There was never any escaping the perception that their winning streak was the result of having him front and center at every game. And while their success had a lot to do with the uncanny talent Bron showed from an early age, there is no getting around the fact that those boys prevailed the way they did because they were a cohesive team.

I knew I could have favored Bron and treated him differently than I did his teammates by giving special privileges. And even though he might have liked that (after all, he was just a kid), I would have eventually lost the support of the team. Instead, I did my best to help my superstar understand he was part of something much bigger than himself and if he valued his teammates over himself by selflessly making them better, he'd always be the kind of player everyone would want on their team.

It was true with Bron, and it's been true with every player I've had who has aimed for service over ego. My most successful teams over the years have been those with players who focused on how they could serve each other as opposed to how they could excel individually.

Selflessness has become the foundation, the bedrock, of my approach as a basketball coach. And it's a two-way street. On the one hand, I strive to check my ego at the door of every gym, arena, or rec center I ever step onto, knowing I'm there not for myself but for the benefit of the kids, and on the other hand, I make it a point to make sure they're also carrying their own air of selflessness, whether doing drills, practicing for a game, or performing on the court. Everyone, from coach to player, needs to operate with the common understanding that we are bound by commitment and fueled by our collective goal.

CHAPTER 8

Make Lemonade

In three words I can sum up everything I've learned about life: it goes on. *Robert Frost*

There's no getting around it. As human beings we're pretty much hardwired to want what we want. We have dreams, goals, intentions, ambitions — and on the good days, we even have decent amounts of determination to move us in the direction of those objectives. We psych ourselves up; we tell ourselves we can do it or that we deserve it. At our best, we struggle through the challenges. We put ourselves out there, dig deep, and aim high.

Then, when we least expect it or are least prepared for it, life or reality or circumstances — call it whatever you will — comes right out of nowhere and smacks us around. Sometimes a little, sometimes a lot. And then that goal, that dream, that target, somehow seems to slip from our grasp like sand through a fist, and we're left wondering if anything ever works out; or worse, we become bitter because things didn't go the way we wanted or expected them to.

I've talked a lot about maximizing opportunities, about staying focused and being disciplined, about the power of being humble and generous of spirit, and about staying true to yourself. But what happens when you do this with lion-like intensity, with every bit of grit you've got, and things still don't work out? What if you have tried every imaginable path to your objective and you seem to be nowhere near it? What's your next move if you've tapped into every last drop of determination, to no avail?

Well, that's when you take orders from that proverbial cliché — and you make lemonade.

We've all heard it before: *When life gives you lemons, you make lemonade,* an adage that employs lemons to depict any less than favorable situation in a person's life. But, of course, a giant spectrum of "bad things" can happen in a person's life to make things feel wrong or negative — scenarios ranging from not making the team, to getting a bad grade, to having an unsightly pimple, to getting fired, to getting a divorce, and at the harsher end of things, something as severe as getting cancer.

EVERYTHING CHANGES

To really get at the heart of what I'm talking about, let's backtrack and look at an insight I believe is crucial because it sums up our whole existence. When I was in college, poring over the various spiritual texts that ultimately led me back to Christendom, I came across a principle Buddhists call "the universal law of impermanence."

This law states that at every second and even every nanosecond, we are changing — and everything, the entirety of the universe, is also always changing. So not only are our insides changing, shifting, growing, receding, expanding, and collapsing, but our realities, the circumstances of our lives, are also always in flux.

One moment, I'm living in East Liverpool as a single man just out of college, with no car and zero direction, and another moment, I'm driving my son and ten other boys around in a van in Akron, with my wife next to me, all of us headed to an important tournament. One day, I'm detoxing off drugs at my sister's place in Queens, and another day I'm in deep meditation, soaking in the words of my pastor at a Sunday service. The only constant (besides me) throughout all this shifting and transforming *is* the shifting and transforming — which teaches us that we have to be ready for anything.

In the good times, the work we put in leads us closer to the destination we foresaw. Someone who is looking to get married, for example, goes on a series of dates for six months or a year and ultimately finds Mr. or Mrs. Right and happily walks down that longed-for aisle. Or someone who's eager to learn Spanish enrolls in a course and walks away a year later speaking the language fluently enough to plan a long visit to Spain.

But for all those sweet moments, inevitably we all have our share of the bitter too, the proverbial lemons — for the simple reason that everything changes. But because we are creatures of habit, we resist these changes, especially when they feel deeply unfavorable. Instead of accepting the fluid nature of life, we tighten up and struggle through these inescapable transitions, especially when the transitions seem to make our life worse. So what happens when the ebb and flow of life brings with it changes that are not positive or, even worse, actually feel terrible? What do we do with the reality we are left with when life's changes feel negative?

As I see it, we only have one choice: We find a way to *make* them positive.

INGREDIENTS FOR LEMONADE

Turning a bad situation into something good is the essence of making lemonade, but unfortunately it never feels as simple as adding a few teaspoons of sugar to lemon juice. Instead, we often get so wrapped up in fear and disappointment over not getting what we want that we're practically blinded from any sense of optimism. But the truth is that there are four ingredients that can turn even the bitterest drink into something sweet and refreshing: acceptance, attitude, effort, and creativity.

Acceptance is the number one ingredient because if we can't accept the things we can't control, we will forever wallow in dissatisfaction. We have to be willing to accept whatever situation life throws at us, because it is in this mind-set of calm understanding — as opposed to suffering in misery — that we can truly begin to craft our other options.

The irony is that while acceptance is a principle I came to understand through Buddhism, it's a strong Christian principle I was exposed to at an early age. I was taught the story of Job in Sunday school. And what is the story of Job if not a study in the power of acceptance. No matter what sort of calamity that comes his way — disease, poverty, even the death of his children — Job ultimately holds on to his faith and refuses to turn away from God. As he says to his wife in Job 2:10, "Shall we accept good from God, and not trouble?"

A less dramatic yet still instructive meditation on the power of acceptance is found in Matthew 6:25 – 27: "I tell you, do not worry about your life, what you will eat or drink; or about your body, what you will wear. Is not life more than food, and the body more than clothes? Look at the birds of the air; they do not sow or reap or store away in barns, and yet your heavenly Father feeds them. Are you not much more valuable than they? Can any one of you by worrying add a single hour to your life?"

Although I've had my moments of anxiety, my journey is definitely a testimony to the power of acceptance. For example, for many years I accepted the reality of working for ConAgra, despite the fact that I truly didn't want to be there. Now you might say, taking home a good paycheck for steady work in corporate America — especially given my humble beginnings — isn't in the same league as the trials that Job underwent. And you won't get any argument from me. But as anyone who has been through it can attest, having an unfulfilling, uninspiring job can produce anxiety. So while I always dreamed of something different, I accepted my job in corporate America as long as it represented my best chance to provide for my family. And in time, God revealed His ultimate plan for me, and I was able to move into my current calling. But it might have never happened if I had rashly acted on my disappointment in corporate America.

Attitude is another crucial ingredient. Having a positive attitude is a great way to energize yourself so that when you struggle to strategize your way out of a "bad" situation, the strategy will be laced with positivity and possibility. It's also another principle deeply rooted in Christian faith. One of the best-known phrases in the Bible, "You of little faith" (Matthew 8:26), is essentially an indictment of those who lack such an attitude. Remember, Jesus says this to His disciples after they convince themselves that their boat is about to capsize. The wind is howling, the waves are coming over the sides, and the disciples are having a really hard time staying positive. But Jesus reminds them that having true faith means believing that even the stormiest seas will eventually calm down. And then He proves it by having the winds die down and the waves subside at His command.

Along with acceptance and a positive attitude, another ingredient for lemonade is *effort*. In chapter 5, we spoke a lot about discipline, which goes hand in hand with effort. Think of discipline as the practice of something, and effort as the personal dose of power you bring to it. It's how much of yourself, your time, and your focus you are willing to give to something in order to exert the change you'd like to see. Effort is your gasoline.

And last but not least, you have to be *creative*. When you're creative, you're able to see past your own preconceptions of how things are or should be and envision a whole new configuration of truths. This gives you new targets to set your eyes on, with a new world of options to explore. It requires stepping outside of your comfort zone and trying to see possibilities you would have never previously imagined.

When the boys started as freshmen at St. Vincent-St. Mary, they were under the seasoned tutelage of Coach Keith Dambrot. Coach Dambrot had just come off a short stint as head coach of Central Michigan University, a Division I school, and he brought an intensity the boys weren't used to. Even though I had prided myself on being a good coach to them until then, I didn't have nearly as much experience as Keith brought to the table, and he wasn't shy about showing them he meant business.

As much as I respected his sense of structure and his hawk-like observational skills, never missing a play anywhere on the court, I wasn't always comfortable with his approach. In particular, I wasn't used to his way of screaming and even sometimes cursing at the kids. I'm not passing any judgment, as every man has his own style or approach, and despite my profound admiration for his coaching methodology (cursing notwithstanding), it wasn't the way I coached.

In many ways, Coach Dambrot's fiery nature was both a gift and a curse. There's no doubt it could ultimately bring out the best in his players. Not surprisingly the boys hated his practices at first, but once we all got past Keith's brash style, we were able to see what was really there: an uncompromising, experienced coach who wanted only good things for the team and the individuals who comprised it.

For two seasons, as the boys (the Fab Four Plus One) skyrocketed, it was Keith who led their way. I know Dru III saw him as a true mentor and probably felt a sense of relief that someone other than his dad was calling the shots. Even Bron, whom Keith was particularly hard on, began to understand the value of his demanding nature.

I was Keith's assistant, and of course I like to believe I played a part in the team's success, having been with these kids since they were very young, but it was truly Keith Dambrot's guidance and tough love that gave that team the ammo it needed to climb the heights by their junior year. They were, as I've told you, unstoppable — and Keith was the one who had set the tone for their dominance.

As the start of their junior season grew closer, the buzz around the team wasn't just of dominating the local competition but of winning the national championship as well. But on the eve of the season, the unimaginable happened: Coach Dambrot told us he wasn't coming back.

After all the hard work of two seasons, which earned them two state championships and ranked them in the top ten during their sophomore year, after how hard the boys had played for him, finishing at 53 – 1, Coach Dambrot decided to take an assistant coaching job at the University of Akron. To say the boys were devastated is a huge understatement.

Some of the boys remember finding out about this devastating piece of news from a reporter, though Keith maintains he told them himself. Bron said he didn't want to speak to or ever see him again. Sian was deeply bitter and suggested that Keith used them to get back to college coaching, claiming that he "sold us up the river." Dru felt straight-up lied to, since he had made his decision to attend STVM believing Coach Dambrot would be there for all of his high school years. I, too, was shocked. The day I found out my wife and I were in the middle of our annual trek through the Akron Parade of Homes. A writer from Cleveland's *Plain Dealer* called to tell me the news.

Later that night when Keith called me, he explained what I already knew: that following the Central Michigan situation, in which he was fired for using a racial term in front of his players, this was his singular chance to get back into college coaching. He also shared with me some of his concerns, which had a lot to do with all the hype buzzing around Bron. Having already been through a media circus when he was dismissed from Central Michigan, he didn't want the kind of spotlight that coaching Bron was sure to bring. He later admitted it was one of the hardest decisions he'd ever made because he would never even have been considered for the University of Akron opportunity if it hadn't been for the players on his STVM team. "Those guys resurrected my career," he said.

My first instinct was to try to convince him it was a terrible idea, that these guys needed him and had so much going for them. I knew how much he wanted to get back to the Division I ranks, but I felt like the timing wasn't right.

Then he said something I really didn't see coming: "I want you to take over." He said he'd already begun discussions with the board at STVM and promised to support me throughout the transition. "Those are your kids," he said. "You're the one who brought them to me." Even though I was speechless for the first few moments of our conversation, I knew deep down he was right. Those boys were a part of my journey, and I was a part of theirs.

But despite having entertained the dream of being a high school coach for a long time, I didn't say yes right away.

Even as Keith pumped me up with promises of guidance and support, a world of doubts swam around in my mind. First and foremost, I didn't think I had enough experience — how could I even come close to matching what Keith brought to the bench? He'd held three college head coaching gigs before coming to STVM; I'd been the head coach of an AAU team.

Perhaps most importantly, the team's junior year schedule was a lot stronger, as they were slated to play against four teams in the top twenty-five nationwide, and they were moving up from Division III in Ohio to Division II. I knew how tough the schedule was going to be because I'd worked with Keith to set it up! And I knew the fans' expectations for us that year were sky-high. Anything short of playing for a national championship would be considered a failure.

I was also worried the boys might be too comfortable with me. As the saying goes, familiarity breeds contempt, and we were definitely familiar. I knew at the end of the day we had each other's backs, but I also considered that this familiarity could backfire on me somehow. The doubts were everywhere. I felt lost.

And again it was the words of my wife that helped me understand a bigger picture.

"Dru," she said, "how can you say no?"

Carolyn made me understand that despite all the fears bubbling up, this moment was God's doing, His way of honoring me for all the years I put in with those boys early on. She reminded me of all the AAU practices and tournaments, of the long car rides and selling duct tape door to door. She reminded me of the principles of life I shared with the boys, principles I never wavered on, even when my command of basketball X's and O's felt shaky. She made me see that this moment was a piece of my sacred responsibility. And as bitter a taste as Coach Dambrot's departure had left in the boys' mouths, Carolyn made me realize this moment was a way to make lemonade out of it.

So rather than focus on my fears, I tried to embrace this opportunity. With Keith gone, I'd be able to step in and do the thing I had been knowingly or unknowingly preparing for. When I finally got my head around what it meant for me personally, those lemons didn't seem so bad after all. And I like to believe the kids felt the same way. Sure, they were hurt and felt dissed, and they hadn't seen Keith's departure coming. But when they started to feel the pleasure of knowing that the guy who was there from the beginning was going to step in to lead them again, there was a sense among all of us that everything really does happen for a reason. I'm not saying the transition was easy, but it's the best we could have done under the circumstances.

We had to (1) accept the fact that Coach Dambrot was out; (2) consciously shift our attitudes from negative to positive, despite our discomfort with this new reality; (3) commit to making our best effort without him, no matter what; and (4) get creative and resourceful about how we were going to prevail. Had we left out any of those steps, we wouldn't have been able to plow forward with strength and focus.

RISING ABOVE INJUSTICE

Perhaps the biggest barrel of lemons came during the "jersey scandal" during the boys' senior year. It seems like ancient history now, but at the time it was national — yes, *national* — news. For those of you who may not remember, on January 25, 2003, Bron visited a clothing store called Next, located in a swanky Cleveland suburb, where a store associate offered him two replica jerseys as gifts — one of former Baltimore Bullets basketball star Wes Unseld and one of Gale Sayers, the legendary former Chicago Bears player. The folks at the store gave those jerseys to him — neither of which Bron particularly wanted or asked for — and also asked him to pose for photos. By now he was used to being in the public eye and typically erred on the side of politeness when it came to these things, so he did what felt most natural when they asked him to pose: he said "sure" and smiled. He was flattered by the gifts, but that was pretty much where he left the whole thing — until a story with said photos ran in the *Plain Dealer* five days later, and all hell broke loose.

An investigation was immediately launched, and within days the Ohio High School Athletic Association decided Bron had violated its amateurism bylaws by "capitalizing on his athletic fame by receiving gifts," which were priced at upward of $800. Apparently, $100 was the maximum dollar amount deemed acceptable by the association. The penalty for this violation? We had to forfeit our January 26 victory over Buchtel and Bron was declared ineligible for the rest of the season. Can you imagine that? Not a fine, not a warning, not a letter of admonishment, nothing. The poor kid, who literally lived and breathed basketball, was told he couldn't play. Here was a kid who made Ohio high school basketball relevant to the outside world, and now our state's high school athletic association turned against him. The whole thing felt just plain wrong.

When Bron first got wind of what felt like the most unjust suspension imaginable, his immediate reaction was not, "Poor me; I can't play" or "Oh no, this is going to ruin my year"; instead, he felt he had somehow betrayed his fellow players. Right away, he thought of his teammates. Even though it was his mess and the spotlight was on him, and even though the jerseys had in fact been gifted to him (and he had no idea of their value at the time of the gifting), he didn't think of himself; he thought of them. He knew the Fab Five had gone into the season dreaming of winning a national championship, and he felt responsible for the dream seemingly leaving their grasp.

Bron wanted to make a personal appeal to the athletic association because he was sure they'd understand what he'd done. So he wrote a letter and poured his heart into it. They had to know that basketball was everything to this young man, that it was going to be the thing that kept him off the streets for his whole life, that he worked diligently in school so he could play for this team, that this sport had saved his life. Bron was sure that if he was candid, apologetic, and respectful, the association would certainly change its mind. But it didn't, and the suspension stood.

This incident sparked one of the few times I saw tears in Bron's eyes, and he wasn't crying for himself alone; he was crying for the whole group. I was infuriated over the injustice of the whole thing, but more than that, I knew I had to do something to help him through it. So I said to him, "If this is the worst thing that happens to you in your life, you will have lived a pretty good life." No one had died. He hadn't blown out a knee or tore an Achilles, putting his future in jeopardy. Shoot, we hadn't even lost a game yet. It was my way of putting the whole thing in perspective and helping him understand that in the grand scheme of things, things could have been a lot worse. I wasn't trying to belittle his pain and disappointment; I was just hoping to expand his point of view. Knowing how much he wanted his team to prevail, I also promised him I would do everything humanly possible to prep the team to play the best basketball it could without him there.

Bron wasn't the only one to contend with. His teammates were beyond crushed too. They felt under attack by the athletic association and by its commissioner, Clair Muscaro, who became the de facto villain behind what they felt was a ridiculous ruling. To them, the association was out to get them. I was a little more sympathetic, as I understood the association was likely getting complaints about the team's unparalleled superstardom and that the commissioner probably felt he had to crack down on us a bit just to show he wasn't playing any favorites.

People were, as a matter of fact, having a hard time wrapping their heads around this idea that Bron, for better or worse, was becoming a national icon. Today we can understand why — he truly is a once-in-a-generation talent and personality. But at the time, it seemed like too much too soon. The media speculated that he was prematurely capitalizing on his name and questioned if he was deserving of the hype (never mind that they were the ones who fueled it in the first place). One journalist said the Bron phenomenon was something the high school system wasn't designed to handle.

The worst part about it was that St. Vincent-St. Mary didn't back up Bron, despite the fact that he had made STVM a household name across the country. It was hard to believe that after all the sacrifices these boys made when they decided to attend STVM instead of Buchtel and how hard they played for the school, the school didn't seem prepared to go to war for Bron with the athletic association. To us, we were feeling like, *Why are we putting ourselves out there for this school?*

Bron would come to practices just to watch, and we could plainly see the tears he'd try to hide. In the media and on the streets, the talk was only about how Bron's suspension was going to derail our season. It was almost a foregone conclusion that the team wouldn't be able to win without him.

The talk was hard to ignore, but Dru, being the little fighter he is, and the rest of the boys were keen on showing everyone how wrong that thinking was. After all, when you're in a heated game of chess, you don't just abandon the game because your knights or bishops, or even your queen, get taken. You play the game until there is a winner at the end of it all. And that's exactly what we decided to do. It wasn't easy to play without our number one man. But at the end of it all, we were more than one man; we were a *team* — a team that had to win, not only for their own sense of power but also for him. There was nothing left to do except to keep on winning.

The first game without Bron was slated against the Bulldogs of Canton McKinley Senior High School, a school known for its strong athletic tradition (no team has been to more Final Fours in Ohio than McKinley). I'm sure they were emboldened by Bron's absence and couldn't wait to get on the court for a showdown against my boys. But my team's dream of playing for a national championship hinged on this game, so we all knew this would be the moment of truth. It would be the chance for the rest of the team to strut its stuff, with or without Bron, showing everyone the value of having a solid group in place. It would be their chance to prove their own talents, which would hopefully silence the naysayers who suggested this team thrived solely off of Bron's talents.

"If we were ever unified, we need to be more unified than ever," I said earnestly in the locker room before the game. "This is the biggest game of the season, because tomorrow is not promised and the past is over; this is all we got right now. This is all we got — RIGHT NOW. We're a great team with a great player. But this is not a one-man show. This is a great TEAM. Don't you ever sell yourself short. I'm just saying words now, but you guys need to go out there and do it on the floor. Play hard, play smart, have fun."

During the game, Bron sat on the bench, wearing a mustard yellow suit that matched our team's uniform colors. He looked sharp and elegant, the subtext likely being, *I will not sulk; I am here for my brothers; I'm not with them out on the court, but I've never been more with them than this moment.* The energy at the University of Akron's Rhodes Arena was palpable, because as much as folks were there to watch the game, I think they were also there to watch Bron watch the game. The question on everyone's mind hung in the air like smog: *Can they do it without him?*

Right from the start, the Bulldogs showed us they were going for the jugular, breaking our press and getting several easy baskets. There were several times when it seemed like our guys might be overmatched. The team was so used to having Bron to fall back on, so this game became a real test of their strength, stamina, basketball IQ, and even their self-esteem.

But Dru had that warrior persona on full throttle and moved around the court during that first period like someone hell-bent on accomplishing a task; he was playing from his place of rage. As Bron's friend, brother, and teammate, he felt that anyone who took a shot at Bron was in essence taking a shot at the whole team. So it appeared he was using his anger to fuel him through the challenge. He had the same look of unyielding determination in his eyes he'd had during his freshman year when he hit those seven three-pointers in a row. He took over the court like it was his and his alone, helping the team to a generous lead in the first quarter. I could feel Bron's satisfaction and pride in his friend.

But the Bulldogs lived up to their name and gave us a real fight, and we had the added handicap of Romeo still recovering from a nasty flu he had been battling. He wasn't able to play his hardest and even had to throw up during some of the time-outs. Even though we had a solid ten-point lead, that age-old saying kept popping into my mind, "Everything changes" — so I thought we'd better be ready if and when things do change on this court.

In the third quarter, we were up 36 – 28, and Romeo seemed to be back in business. Dru had given him one of his "tough love" pep talks during halftime, some of which must have sunk in, because Romeo's hard work left the team with a lead going into the last quarter. Flu or no flu, Romeo's energy in the fourth quarter maintained our double-digit lead at 60 – 50. Despite a few three-pointers from the Bulldogs, we managed to hold on to win 63 – 62.

Yes, having Bron out was a lemon of epic proportions. But the sweet lemonade came in the form of letting the rest of the guys prove to themselves and to the world that their success did not hinge on one player but was the result of being an amazing *team*.

After the pressure of that game was off and Bron could think about things calmly, he decided to take matters into his own hands.

After all, he knew in his heart he hadn't done anything wrong, that whatever had happened that day in the store was beyond him, and that receiving a couple of shirts as gifts was certainly no crime. He was a hardworking kid on and off the court, kept his grades up while playing, and always rose above any slanderous talk or rumors about him. And even if accepting those shirts was against the rules in any way, he felt the penalty didn't match the violation, so together with his mother, they focused on figuring out a way to get the ruling overturned.

The problem was that in many ways, the ruling had a personal element to it, as St. Vincent-St. Mary had been having a beef with the athletic association for a while. I myself had been feeling animosity from Clair Muscaro, who alleged that I had once walked off the court cursing. I don't have to remind you how I feel about cursing, so not only was this allegation plainly false; it also gave me a window into the kind of mind-set I'd be up against.

There was also the fact that Muscaro had publically taken issue with the team's robust schedule that took them throughout the country for games against nationally ranked teams. He was of the belief (and not afraid to say so) that our games should be largely local, that we shouldn't be so grandiose. He didn't realize that by that point, we had no competition left in Ohio, so if we wanted to improve, we had no choice but to leave our comfort zone. Maybe he also didn't realize that these kids had a dream.

With the support of his mother, LeBron decided to enlist the aid of a lawyer from Cleveland, the same one who had helped them through an ordeal related to an expensive Hummer that Bron's mother gave him on his eighteenth birthday. A couple of days after the Canton McKinley game, the lawyer, Frederick Nance, filed a motion for a temporary restraining order and preliminary injunction on Bron's behalf to stop the association from revoking his eligibility. But Clair Muscaro refused to budge.

The main problem with the accusation the association was

holding over Bron's head was the claim that *he* was trying to capitalize on his celebrity status as an athlete when the real culprits trying to do this were the media outlets that scavenged for scandalous stories about him like a school of hungry sharks. No one at the association seemed to understand that if Bron had really wanted to capitalize, he would have accepted deals with eager athletic shoe companies and dropped out of school to run his own show. He could have done that at any point. But he was there to play ball with his boys. Nobody seemed to get that as famous as LeBron James was at this point, he still had the heart of a servant when it came to his team.

And after the team's fall from grace during their junior year, they weren't about to give up their dream over a couple of jerseys.

Thanks to Bron's decision to grab the bull by the horns and defend himself, things turned around. On February 5, with swarms of reporters waiting to hear the verdict, a Summit County judge ruled that Bron's eligibility be immediately restored. According to the judge, the punishment for the infraction seemed too severe, and as of that day, he'd be reinstated. Finally.

The two conditions were that Bron would still be ineligible for one game, which STVM could choose, and that the forfeit of our game against Buchtel would be upheld. Neither of these two clauses bothered any of us — honestly, we were just happy to have our man back.

Even though it came late, we were glad to see that even the school ultimately came out in support of Bron. Before the judge's ruling, James Burdon, the chairman of the board of trustees at STVM, said, "Our support of Bron is because of who he is. He's a member of the school community here. In his years as a student at STVM, he has excelled academically and socially, as well as athletically. As part of our school community, he deserves our wholehearted support."

Of course we were all delighted with the way things turned out, and even more than that, I knew it would only light the fires of vindication in Bron. I was fully aware he had every intention of coming back onto that court with guns blazing, so to speak.

Our first game after the ruling was against Los Angeles-based Westchester High School, which we played in Trenton, New Jersey. At first it seemed like the boys were ready to let it rip, feeling relaxed and happy about having the team intact. But somehow Westchester managed to rev up to a quick six-point lead. It didn't last long, however, with Romeo scoring the first two points for us and Bron swooping in with a solid 18 points that put us cleanly in the lead after the first quarter. By halftime, he had 31 points, and by the end of the game he was at 52, which was not only his career high but also the opposing team's *entire* score for the game, with STVM victorious at 78 – 52. He came onto that court like a bull that'd been corralled for too long, playing with his usual deftness and then some.

SAVOR THE LEMONADE

Through it all, we managed to make lemonade out of life's lemons. In spite of the crushing loss during their junior year; in spite of losing Coach Dambrot, who was a key figure for the team and also for me; in spite of losing Bron for two games, we were able to prevail and hurdle all the obstacles placed in front of us.

However, the scrutiny of the team and me never stopped. Years later, I'd go online and find comments about how the team's success was a result of my white assistant coach, which gives me a big laugh, knowing the race element always seems to find a way to creep into everything.

And the boys would have to deal with always being in the spotlight, for better or worse, and until they'd graduate, they would be the target of gossip and criticism for this or that reason. At first they were targeted because they chose STVM over Buchtel. Then when they'd given their hearts to STVM, they'd be targeted for becoming too successful. They couldn't escape the fact that their stardom seemed to be both a blessing and a curse.

But instead of sulking through the moments of hardship, we buckled down and focused. When we lost Keith, we were shocked and displeased. But when we gave it some thought and put our emotions aside, we realized that no coach (not Keith and not me or anyone else, for that matter) held the fate of this team. Their success would have to be the result of their hard work, determination, and ability to withstand even the most intense changes.

And that test really came when they lost Bron and managed to win without him. Losing Keith as juniors and Bron during their senior year at both points felt like the worst possible things that could happen — lemons of the bitterest kind. In fact, these losses only helped to strengthen the team's resolve and showed them and anyone watching that they were tough enough to handle anything. I certainly stepped up to the challenge of being a head coach, which if I'm honest, was the dream of my life. As for the boys, they grew even closer, worked even harder, and became even more determined to accomplish their dreams — which would ultimately be the sweetest lemonade of all.

CHAPTER 9

Take Charge of
Your Own Mind

Change your thoughts, and you change your world.

Norman Vincent Peale

Remember that voice we spoke about a few chapters ago? The pesky, relentless little voice — as opposed to the still, small voice of the heart — that creeps into our thoughts and hunkers down and sets up shop in there like it owns the place? This endlessly chattering voice is our inner monologue that fills the space of our internal world and, to a large extent, determines not only how we feel but also how we perceive things and how we act. Looked at this way, our whole existence — thoughts, feelings, and behavior — is predicated on how we navigate our sometimes volatile and often unpredictable inner monologue.

It doesn't take a psychologist or neuroscientist to understand the basic premise that if our thoughts are laced with the negative, then negativity will find a way to seep into our mind-set and inevitably bleed into how we behave. This is why the *tone* of our thoughts is so crucial.

Think about it. If we played a recording all day long that contained nothing but the sound of harsh static or shrill sirens or constant banging, by the end of the day we'd feel terrible and want to rip out our hair. We'd feel assaulted somehow, and our brains would yearn for peace and quiet. While this is an extreme example, it gives some indication of what happens when we lose the reins of our own mental processes and allow our minds to be filled with all kinds of negative thoughts.

Thankfully, the opposite is true too. If we load our minds with positive thoughts, then positivity will have no choice but to overflow into our disposition and, in turn, directly into our actions. To use a counterexample, if we spend a day listening to the sounds of waterfalls or babbling brooks or waves lapping rhythmically onto a shore, it's likely that at the end of the day our minds will be calm. There's a reason recordings can be found for those seeking aural serenity. In both of these examples, certain sounds depict types of thoughts and cause us to think about the quality of our inner voice. The calmer, the better; the more jarring, the more challenging.

While negativity and positivity are opposites, they have something in common — their uncanny and powerful ability to dictate the flow of a person's life. The Bible tells it straight in Philippians 4:8 – 9: "Finally, brothers and sisters, whatever is true, whatever is noble, whatever is right, whatever is pure, whatever is lovely, whatever is admirable — if anything is excellent or praiseworthy — think about such things. Whatever you have learned or received or heard from me, or seen in me — put it into practice. And the God of peace will be with you."

It sounds simple enough in theory, right? *Just don't have bad thoughts.* But the reality of doing this feels like one of the great paradoxes of humanity. This enigma may have something to do with the fact that our thoughts are not tangible or visible and only exist in the confines of our own brains, so maybe we unintentionally give them a sense of fluidity and allow them to swirl around unwatched. Moreover, some of our thoughts happen in the subconscious realm, so how can we ever exert any control over those, right? How bad can something be if you can't even see or touch it, right? Or how can something so abstract be harmful to me or others in any way?

I've already talked at length about meditation and how powerful this tool can be to quiet the mind. But now I'd like to take it a few steps further and explore other avenues as we do the hard work of digging deep and really *taking charge of our minds*.

If you think about it, the mind, left to its own devices, is like an unruly, untamed beast. It wants what it wants; it leaps abruptly and vehemently from one idea to the next; and it has enough strength to weigh a person down. This beast can be aggressive, clumsy, unclear in its motivations, and downright troublesome.

But here's the flip side. We've all seen big dogs that, despite their size and stature, walk dutifully behind their master, with the knowledge that it's indeed their master who leads the way and calls the shots. This calm beast does not pounce; he does not howl; he does not pull the master this way or that. He is instead led by the master down a path that makes sense, and no matter what may be bothering this beast, he walks where the master walks — obedient and trusting. Such are the qualities of a mind kept in check.

Ideally, we are the masters of our minds, and not vice versa, just like a master who walks his dog, and not the opposite. Even the word *master* connotes the idea that *this person* is the one in charge. In a perfect world, we are able to dictate where our thoughts will go and how much power and control they will have on us. In such a world, our intangible, abstract thoughts are not unlike our very tangible external limbs — controlled by us and us alone.

But it often feels like we are under the spell of the mind, somehow slaves to our own selves. Besides sitting quietly on a regular (ideally daily) basis and observing our internal world with intention, what are some other ways we can become masters of our mind?

CONTROL WHAT YOU CAN CONTROL

I'm sure you've heard this plea (referred to as the Serenity Prayer in many twelve-step recovery programs): "God, grant me the serenity to accept the things I cannot change, the courage to change the things I can, and the wisdom to know the difference." This concept, usually expressed as a personal supplication, is the art of what I like to call *controlling what you can control* — something every person should aim to master if they are serious about taking charge of their minds.

But *how* do we do this? How can we put this concept into everyday use? I believe it begins with the steadfast practice of turning inward and focusing on the things we *can* control, which are our thoughts, perceptions, attitudes, and actions.

You'll notice I didn't include the word *feelings* on this list, because to a certain degree, we really cannot control our feelings. It can happen, as we all know, that we wake up feeling a little mournful or depressed one morning, and we may not even know why. And certainly if something tragic or sad happens in our lives, the feelings that accompany such events are what they are — painful. But while we may not be able to control our feelings, what we *can* do is observe them. We can watch them as they happen inside us, watch them pass and change, and even watch new ones crop up, knowing a crucial truth the whole time: that feelings are not facts.

So let's get back to those things we can control: our thoughts, perceptions, attitudes, and actions. How do we keep our focus on those? Proverbs 4:25 – 26 says it best: "Let your eyes look straight ahead; fix your gaze directly before you. Give careful thought to the paths for your feet and be steadfast in all your ways."

We have an individual duty to keep our eyes fixed on our purpose, to identify the pathways to those objectives, and to use our lives to make those everyday treks. Because when we live in line with our purpose, we are like a flower that blossoms fully each day, and when we don't, we live in a permanent state of being wilted. By staying focused on the things we dream of and that make us happy, we allow less room for the neurotic voice. By filling our consciousness with thoughts and ideas about how to make our dreams come true, we stamp out the fires of doubt and fear. When we use our energy for making progress in our lives, we leave less energy in our reservoir for anguish.

Yes, it all sounds great on paper. But life and reality are not lived as words in a book, and the mind's unsolicited takeover happens to all of us, probably multiple times a day or even every hour. Trust me when I say I've had to work insanely hard to take charge of my mind, especially in the context of coaching teenage boys.

Many personalities and factors penetrate each workout, each practice, every team, and every game, and I find myself having to constantly maintain control so as to not add to the situation with my own burst of rage. Sometimes there's a kid who loves to talk back or a ref who seems keen on making questionable calls or a know-it-all parent who thinks he can run my team better than me or an opposing team that comes onto the court with a little too much aggression in their eyes. What do all these things have in common? They are all external circumstances, which means they are *outside of me* — which means I cannot control them.

Instead of getting bent out of shape over variables that exist beyond me, I tell myself to rein in that energy and channel it toward something that lives within me — such as my spiritual commitment to live a Christian life or my professional goal of teaching young kids how to collaborate as a team or my intention to be a loving husband and father. An ineffective me, one consumed by outside forces, would stomp around in anger, huffing and puffing and carrying on about the injustices I'm facing. A more effective me, however, sees there isn't enough anger in the world to change these things and will instead exert every bit of my mental power toward keeping my goals and values clear.

Rather than cursing out that annoying ref or getting into an argument with a meddling parent, I'll take a deep breath and take stock of what I need to be doing for the sake of my own ongoing agendas. In this way, I diffuse seemingly bad situations with the power of my own conviction. Sometimes it's harder than other times. Given the notoriety of the team, Bron's ascension to superstardom, and the sheer momentum that came with it, as coach, I was front and center for the media to devour. And devour they did, often leaving me scratching my head, enraged by their scrutiny, thinking to myself, "Dang, I'm just a high school coach."

But in order to lead, I'd have to shake it off and remind myself I was indeed the coach of a prominent team, and that as honorable and fulfilling as it could be, it came at the price of my anonymity. I'd have to shelve hurt feelings, or at least observe them without identifying with them too closely, and realize that part of being the coach of a high-profile team meant being in the path of the media's point of view more often than I cared to be.

I'd have to accept the idea that when it comes to my profession, the long-standing perception is that the players are the ones who win games, and the coaches are the ones who lose them. Even though I've always known this, I make it a point to remind myself of its truth every morning. I'm proud to say my STVM teams have won three state championships, but I also understand that every loss brings a new invitation to be second-guessed and questioned. Which is why I walk into a practice or a game armed with the realities of what it means to be a coach etched into my awareness, so that when things slip from my grasp, I have a rational point of reference to which I can always return. Coaching has given me a crash course on the art of letting things go.

We can get so strung out because things aren't happening the way we envisioned. But that's life. There are many things we didn't plan for; other things we wish had happened differently. But we've still got to move forward — mainly because the goal can still be achieved. And if we work through it and make sacrifices, at the end of the day, even if we don't accomplish the goal, we'll be better for trying.

SET YOUR OWN COURSE

You know what else you can control? Your trajectory. Your path. The route toward your destiny. It's not enough to just let things go and shrug things off or to brush the dust off your shoulders and stand proud of who you are. Ultimately, you still have to go out there and execute. Learning how to let go is one piece; the other part — taking action that's in line with your goals and values — matters just as much. To really be in control, you have a responsibility to put yourself in the driver's seat, leading the expedition of your own life in the direction that makes the most sense to *you*.

As I mentioned earlier, sometimes the close relationships in our lives can dampen the path toward our happiness. It's not that our friends or loved ones don't want us to succeed; they just see the world differently at any given moment or have their own big picture in mind. Too many times I've encountered young men whose dream is to become Division I college basketball players. And when they're around me, they're doing the work to help make that dream a reality. They're practicing hard, working out, studying film, and keeping up their grades. But when they're around their friends, it's a different story. Their friends often don't share the same dreams. Or if they do, those dreams are rooted in little more than a fantasy, a lifestyle they've seen in videos and heard in songs but is, in reality, almost impossible to realize. At least in a healthy manner. So even if I spend five afternoons and a weekend morning each week working with a player on his college dream, a group of friends with a different agenda can undermine it very quickly.

I've seen this scenario play out many times. A few examples continue to haunt me, because I wish I could have helped a young person see more clearly that his friends were leading him down the wrong path. I think of one young man who came to our program from a neighborhood across town. Had he stayed at his neighborhood school, he would have been the star of the team from the moment he stepped on the court. At STVM, he'd have to work harder to achieve that status, but he had the potential to be an outstanding player. Playing for a nationally recognized program like STVM's, he was in a prefect setting to showcase his talent to Division I teams across the country.

Unfortunately, his friends back in his neighborhood didn't see things the same way. They saw him fighting for top billing at STVM and told him I was making a mistake, that he should come back to the hood and be "the man" at his local school. At first he didn't listen to them and remained focused on the plan we had laid out for him at STVM, but eventually those friends wore him down. Despite the fact that a few colleges were showing interest in him, he transferred back to his old school. Yes, he was "the man" there and scored a lot of points, but he didn't progress as a player. His skill set never improved, despite playing against lesser competition, and those colleges lost interest. Instead of going to school on a scholarship, he stayed back on the block with his friends. There was talk of going to junior college so he could get back on the recruiting radar, but in the end it was never anything but talk. By his early twenties, when he should have been graduating from college and entering the job market with a degree from a top school, he was serving time in jail.

Another player met a similar fate. He came from one of the tougher neighborhoods in the area, and I'd known him since he was in fourth grade. He had to deal with a lot of baggage — family members caught up in drugs and adults in his life going in and out of jail. But he was a talented player who worked hard in school, and eventually he came to STVM. Socially, it was a much different environment. He'd come from a largely poor African-American neighborhood, while STVM was predominately white and middle-class. Yet despite the differences, he was able to build friendships with other kids at the school and improve as a player.

He was a funny and charming kid, and people at STVM genuinely liked him. But rather than commit himself fully to making the most of the opportunities that going to a school like STVM provided, he tried to keep a foot in the street culture he had come from. He was more interested in impressing his street friends with how he "got over" on the rich kids at STVM than in doing the work and making the connections that might help him become rich one day.

I have no doubt that had he stayed the course and applied himself, both as a player and a student, one of those rich kids' parents or alumni from the school would have looked out for him and helped him find a job. Instead, he drifted back to the streets, where, despite what his friends were saying, no one was looking out for him. He never finished college and ultimately ended up in jail.

And it's not always as tragic a situation as a kid from the streets winding up in jail. I had a player who came from a suburban school and a middle-class background. He was a very strong player and was on track to get a scholarship offer from a major college program. But he missed his friends at his old school and kept saying he wanted to go back so he could be around them. They weren't kids caught up in street life, but they weren't particularly focused either. This player was good, but in order to be great, he needed to focus on building his skills set.

He ultimately decided to go back to his old school and, predictably, spent more time hanging with his friends than working on his game. The interest from the major schools quickly dried up, and a kid who I thought would have fifteen to twenty scholarship offers to choose from ended up with only one. While this doesn't sound like a tragedy — he still got a scholarship — I wish he could have seen that if his friends really had his best interest at heart, they'd have encouraged him to stay in the best situation for him.

It hurt every time I watched a player suffer because they wouldn't cut ties with their friends. I grew up on the streets too, and I understand the bonds are hard to break. But I also know you're never going to achieve what you're capable of in life when you allow voices from your past to control your future.

This is why when I say, "Learn to let it go," I'm not just talking about negative thoughts or incidents. Unfortunately, sometimes you have to let go of anyone who is consistently nonsupportive, who tries to distract you from your goals, who challenges your objectives, and who makes you feel bad about your choices. That may sound harsh, but I encourage you to see it as a way of pruning your own garden so your soul has room to grow.

As a coach and mentor to young people, I often remind them this is their journey — and theirs alone. "You're not here because of me," I say. "You're not here because of your parents or your friends. You're here because you want to be here. And if I accept the notion that you really want to be here, then you've got no choice but to show it to me. No — you've got to show it to *you*."

It's crucial they realize how distinct each person's journey is, each one packed with factors and circumstances that give it character and direction. It's already hard enough to know what our path should be, and often the process of elimination begins with taking some distance from any relationship that is blurring the way.

I try to tell my kids to accept the fact that relationships will come and go. After all, we're social creatures who will always, for better or worse, have groups, tribes, cliques, clans, circles, and networks of people to whom we cling for this or that reason. Whole new casts of characters are encountered at the start of new school years or on day one of a new job — and then, of course, there are those who have been around throughout our lives. But we all grow in different directions, and more often than not, we are forced to re-root.

This concept is hard for young people to grasp because they tend to give a value to their friendships and peers that outweighs the value of their own dreams. Therefore, as I said earlier, they sometimes allow themselves to stay stuck. Instead of soaring toward their own potential, the comfort of what they already know swallows them up. Please don't get me wrong; I'm not saying relationships are not meaningful. But remember what I said before about everything changing? Well, relationships are no different; they are subject to the ebb and flow of life just like anything else, and when our relationships aren't flexible enough to meet the criteria of our ongoing purpose, they end up falling into the category of excess baggage.

In any field, once you decide you want to pursue your goal, you have to make sacrifices. Some kids just couldn't pull themselves away from their old neighborhood — the very neighborhood that pulled them down. They get sucked into a vortex where ambition doesn't compute and where the cool thing is to do nothing. Whatever little sliver of promise they had inside gets hijacked by the distractions of this static, dead space. But as great as it is to take your friends with you as you move down the road of success, you also must recognize that relationships can be but aren't always for a lifetime. And sometimes your "friends" really play the, "Oh, you're too good for us now" card. When that happens, you have to separate yourself and say, "No, I'm not too good for you. I'm just going in a different direction."

I like to remind kids that you can never really leave a true friend behind, because if they're real friends, they will never try to impede your journey. They will instead develop right alongside you and at the very least encourage and support you. Real friends become your number one fans — and that's as true for us adults as it is for kids.

When it comes to letting things go, it works the other way too. People sometimes come into our lives who we at first want nothing to do with and who seem to simply get in our way. It's only later — perhaps in hindsight — that we realize these particular individuals were meant to come into our lives for a significant reason.

Take Romeo Travis, for example. When he joined the team as a transfer student during the team's sophomore year, he was not yet the proverbial "Plus One." He was a difficult young man — part rebel, part loner, and all grit. He used to refer to himself as "angry man," for which I can't really blame him, as he had a tough upbringing and was still working through it.

It was also rough for Romeo to join a group of boys who were so close they were like brothers. They had their own lingo, their inside jokes, their way of interacting with one another and with the world around them; they were a tiny universe unto themselves.

Romeo's attitude presented the Fab Four with a dilemma. On the one hand, they couldn't stand this newcomer who was unsettling the balance of their perfect little foursome. However, as much as they didn't appreciate his swagger or intimidation tactics, they very much liked his game.

Romeo showed his rare abilities as a ballplayer during one of our most important games of the sophomore year. Our opponent was Buchtel, the African-American school the boys had been expected to attend as freshmen and where they (and I) had a lot of enemies for having chosen the largely white St. Vincent-St. Mary instead. This was the first game against Buchtel since the boys made the decision not to attend, so, needless to say, emotions were running high in the James Rhodes Arena that night. I don't know if it was the pressure or the built-in antagonism of this particular game, but the boys just didn't have their groove. By the end of the second quarter, the score was 37 – 36 in Buchtel's favor, and all of us were feeling like the weight of a loss was already on our shoulders.

That's when Bron and Romeo kicked into high gear as they each hit back-to-back baskets to help us regain the lead and our groove. We ended up winning 58 – 50 — and a lot of it had to do with Romeo's big push at the end. At six foot six, Romeo was an excellent offensive player, with powerful low-post moves and great leaping ability that allowed him to catch countless lob passes from Bron, who was already proving himself an all-time great in the assist department. Romeo also used that leaping ability to control the game as a shot blocker, which led to fast breaks and plenty of memorable dunks from Bron. So despite their off-court differences, on the court Romeo was exactly what the team needed. And they all (including Bron) knew it.

This was a case of the team having no choice but to collectively take charge of their mind and accept Romeo for what he was — a huge asset to the team. If, in fact, their number one priority was the team, they'd have to lay aside the off-court issues with Romeo for the sake of the group's success. They'd have to dig into their own sense of empathy and try to understand Romeo's point of view as a kid who grew up in a poor, fatherless setting and was never part of anything until he was a part of this team.

Romeo would also have to let go of the belief that he was destined to forever be an outsider. He'd have no choice but to soften up a bit and not be intensely brash all the time (even though I always knew this front was his own kind of cry for help). Ultimately, Romeo would have to be a team player if he wanted to be a player on the team.

And in the end, that's what happened. Romeo became the Plus One to the Fab Four and shared enough glory and fond memories with those boys that they're still close today. In fact, during the height of speculation during Bron's second free agency, Bron made headlines by making an appearance during one of the games at his skills academy in Las Vegas. And who did he take the court with? Dru and Romeo.

They're all older and more mature today, but they still deserve tremendous credit for refusing to get stuck in a negative situation years ago. They went from literally pummeling each other on and off the court to working together to teach young boys about the game. Look how far this relationship has come — all because they put their pettiness aside and took charge of their minds.

THE PARENT TRAP

Unfortunately, friends aren't the only ones who get in the way of things. Sometimes it's the adults — parents even — who, despite having the best intentions, find a way to muck things up. Earlier, I spoke about the know-it-all parent, but the parent variable can be unintentionally detrimental to kids in many ways. And let me preface this by saying I'm no exception.

I've already told you about how difficult it was to manage my role as father alongside that of coach when it came to my relationship with my son Dru. There were times when I pushed my son so hard that he ended up in tears — times when I had to ask myself if I was going too far, demanding too much. Ultimately, I reconciled my toughness on him in these two ways: he loved this game more than anything in his life, and we both had to prove our skill set to ourselves and to everyone watching, regardless of our father-son ties. Dru had to be good enough consistently to earn his court time so people wouldn't think he was getting playing time because of me. As petty as it may sound, it was a reality we faced every day. I made plenty of missteps during the period, but as we look back, both of us can say the stumbles were worth the incredible journey we've experienced through basketball.

Then, of course, there are my players' parents. God bless them, as I know all they really want is what most parents want — a good experience for their child. Yet, in their zeal to bring this about, they don't realize they are doing a disservice to the child (as I may have done with Dru on more than one occasion) by pressing them too hard or creating expectations that are either not in line with the child's own dream or simply unattainable.

Some parents are too quick to push their children toward athletics, in the delusion that the next LeBron James is living in their house. Instead of seeing the game for what it is — *a game* — they see a potential cash cow. The essence of the whole thing — the love of the game — fades in this environment because the motivation to excel is not coming from the right place. As a result, kids feel overpressured and are worked too hard rather than being allowed to carve out their authentic place in the world.

The problem often begins when parents view their child's athletic career through a clouded lens. Maybe basketball was the kid's dream when he was nine or ten years old. But now that he's fifteen, he isn't as passionate anymore. He'd rather hang out with his friends or pursue other interests. But parents still push them. Why? Because they want to live that dream *through* the child.

Too many times, I've met young people who have been forced to follow other people's dreams instead of pursuing what truly inspires them. Indeed, I've coached many players whose hearts weren't in basketball, yet they were forced to play the game because their parents loved the game. Or even simply because they were tall. I encourage such players to make the most out of their time playing basketball, but I also let them know they'll be happiest pursuing whatever their true passion is. I also counsel parents to accept their child's passion, even if it doesn't match their own. I believe parents need to nurture their children's dreams, even if they don't (or especially if they don't) echo their own.

All parents should ask themselves, "Am I really nurturing this kid's passion and gifts? Am I paying attention to what's truly important to him or her?" First and foremost, parents should expose their kids to a wide variety of activities and then allow them to gravitate to what excites them. Then when you recognize what excites them, you feed that. I see it with my grandson. I'm a coach, so naturally he's always been around the program but has never shown much interest in basketball. He likes robots. So maybe he wants to be an engineer. If that turns out to be the case, he should go to an engineer camp, not a basketball camp. Do those things that will grow the genius that inherently lives in them rather than force something on them that doesn't light their fire. All kids have a spark, and if we can find and light it in our children, we'll be much better off as a society.

Everyone has their own parenting style, and I'm not here to impose my own ideology. However, since I work with kids and young adults on a regular basis, I've come to see that they shine the brightest when they are in touch with their most authentic sense of self.

In my own case, because football was my first love, I was never a parent who pushed my own kids toward basketball too strongly. But as I've said, once I sensed how dedicated Dru was to the game, I gave him, and later Cameron, all of my support. I had to ask myself some tough questions when neither Dru nor Cameron were highly recruited out of high school. For a moment I thought I could have done things differently. There are coaches out there who change their approach when one of their own kids is on the team. Instead of putting their team in the best position to win, their emphasis becomes putting their kid in the best position to succeed, namely, to score a lot of points so they'll attract the attention of college scouts. I was inclined to do the opposite. I was so worried about people crediting Dru or Cameron's playing time to nepotism that I probably cost them opportunities. When college scouts didn't come knocking, initially I had a crisis of faith and asked myself, *Could I have done more for my sons, even if it was at the expense of other kids entrusted to my care?* The moment passed, and I never went that route. I knew that even if it brought a little shine to my sons, it wasn't the right way for them to grow into the game. I always wanted them to know that if this is something they love, they're going to excel because of the time they put in that will make them exceptional and not because I cleared the path for them.

That's why early on I said to them, "This is your dream. It's not my dream. I'm going to facilitate and help, but in the end, it's your dream. When you don't want to do the work that's required, don't blame me. But if you're willing to do the work, I'll help you. But don't forget: it's *your* dream."

Some parents just don't get it and can't shake the fact that it's really their own dream for their child to excel in sports. To me, that's a recipe for disaster — one that will inevitably bring with it resentment and shoddy effort, not to mention the fact that it will divert the child from his true calling.

I see this happen a lot with children of former athletes. Because Mom or Dad used to be pretty good at the game, these kids are often blessed with a tantalizing combination of height and ability. Because their parents loved the game, they'll push their own kids toward it — with pretty good results at first. But just because you loved the game doesn't mean your kid is going to love it too, even if he or she is good at it. Think about it; how many of us want to pursue the same things our parents did? Probably not too many of us.

While every parent may feel the urge to tell their child what career path to choose or which person to marry, ultimately they must accept the fact that those decisions are out of their control. That part of the parental mind is very hard to control, but it must be mastered for both the parents' and child's sake. As a parent, you've got to let go of that desire to control the destination of your children's lives and have faith that the example you have set over the years will steer them in the right direction, no matter where that journey leads.

Another problem I see all the time is the inordinate number of families that underemphasize academics, which is a real disgrace because it's almost always in the child's best interest to put academics first. I don't mean to sound like a broken record, but there's only one Bron.

I should know, because having coached him I've become something of a magnet to young men (and their parents) who believe they're the next one. And while I've been fortunate to coach some pretty great players since Bron left STVM, none have come close to duplicating his ability. They would have been better off putting academics first. And that's not a knock against anyone's game but rather a cold, unemotional assessment of the realities. Unless you're in the 1 percent skill set basketball wise, you probably have ten to twenty more times earning potential by staying academically focused. As odd as it sounds coming from a basketball coach, when you put all your eggs in the sports basket, you greatly limit your child's potential.

Now if you have a child who really wants to be out there on the court, striving to be the best they can, showing the same dedication and drive that Dru showed me, then you need to support them. But you must also understand that sometimes the best way to provide support is to get out of the way. That might sound counterintuitive, but hear me out. If you've gotten behind your kid's dream of excelling in the game of basketball and shown support by encouraging them to join a team and be a part of a group with a designated leader — in this case, a coach — then part of your duty as the supportive parent is to step aside and let the leader lead.

As much as I talk about the kids having to understand they're part of something greater than themselves, it's equally important that their parents also grasp this notion. This one is tricky because most parents are so innately compelled to defend or advocate for their child that they quickly lose sight of the bigger picture — and the bigger picture has nothing to do with their individual child; it has everything to do with the team as a whole.

I worry sometimes that if parents continue at the pace they're on, we may see a day when no one wants to coach anymore. It's difficult to try to work with a child *you* can see hasn't fully developed his skill set, but *his parents* somehow haven't seen that. I am constantly encountering parents who are quick to complain about playing time for kids who even a casual observer can see don't deserve it yet. I've even had parents question my integrity and challenge my Christian values, for no other reason than that I don't play their son. Even after a win, which should be an upbeat time for everyone on the team and everyone connected to it, I often have to deal with unhappy mothers and fathers. Even if they won't confront me directly, it gets back to me. Parents or uncles tell the kids, "That coach is holding you back; he's sitting on your game."

I've even had parents who videotape at games only when their son is on the floor. Or they keep stats only for their kid and not for the rest of the team. What sort of lesson is that? In my view, it sends the kid a bad message. It says only your numbers are important and, worse, that only *you* are important — which is the total opposite of what I teach.

This is why I always tell the kids, "You have to go home and tell your parents they need to respect the goals of the team." I make sure they stress the idea, *It's not about me; it's about the team. And I'm going to do what's right for the team.* In the best-case scenario, parents will realize that what we're doing has nothing to do with individual ego and everything to do with a unified experience. And those parents will ultimately appreciate such lessons for their kids.

As coaches and leaders, we must employ a razor-sharp focus — a taking charge of our own mind. That's what brings out the best in people of all ages.

COMPARISON AND THE THEORY OF RELATIVE FILTH

If we're going to tackle the question of how to take charge of our own minds, another crucial lesson is to avoid comparing ourselves to others. Every human being is a universe unto himself — each with their own set of circumstances, criteria, thoughts, feelings, reactions, upbringing, geography, physicality, and more. Because all of us are so fundamentally different, comparing ourselves to others is futile and, as such, a monumental waste of our time and energy.

Many recruiters overlooked my youngest son Cameron because of his height, and he struggled with accepting the fact that players he had outperformed were gaining scholarships to top colleges. He used to get upset and say things like, "But I gave that guy the business when we were matched up. How could he get an offer over me?" Or, "I locked that guy down when we played. He had one of his worst games of the season against me. Why are they more interested in him?" But while it was easy to understand Cameron's frustration, ultimately he had to understand he wasn't gaining anything by worrying about someone else's situation. Maybe it *wasn't* fair. Who knows what the reasons were? But any energy put into stewing over those questions was ultimately wasted energy, which is why it was only after Cameron changed his attitude and stopped worrying about what other players were doing and poured all his energy into his own effort that he earned a scholarship to play basketball at Northwood University, a Division II school in Midland, Michigan, and is now an assistant coach there.

And just as we should avoid comparing ourselves to others who seem to be prevailing in a way we're not, we have the same obligation to not allow others' negativity to be our justification for our own negative behavior or attitude.

Years ago, I attended a program called Character Counts, which is centered around six pillars: trustworthiness, respect, responsibility, fairness, caring, and citizenship. In this program I learned about the doctrine of relative filth, which is essentially a type of rationalization used by people to minimize their moral deficiencies by comparing themselves to others who show even lower standards.

Just because someone else is dirty with their actions doesn't give you the right to behave in a similar manner. Many people attempt to rationalize their misdeeds or shortcomings by pointing to their peers and claiming, "Well, it's not as bad as what *they're* doing," or "I did what I did because of what they did." This happens with my players all the time. If I reprimand one of them for not getting back on defense, instead of simply saying, "Got it, Coach," they'll reply, "Well, John didn't get back either. How come you're not saying anything to him?" I have to explain to them that John's shortcomings don't have anything to do with theirs. Maybe I've already had the same conversation with John. Or maybe I told John I wanted him crashing the offensive boards, which makes it harder for him to get back on defense. I might have any number of reasons, but none of them should affect the message I'm giving to the player I singled out.

This is a difficult concept for a lot of kids to grasp because they don't see their own parents taking responsibility. It isn't modeled behavior. They don't see their parents standing up enough and saying, "I was wrong. That wasn't the best thing to do." And when you don't see something modeled, how can you make it a part of who you are? As parents, we must have the confidence to say, "I was wrong."

Sadly, we see a lot of finger-pointing in American culture. All we have to do is take a quick look at the political stage to see the blame game in full swing. Like I always tell my guys, whenever you point a finger, there are three of them pointing right back at you. In other words, each of us must take responsibility for our own actions.

As I continue to grow as a coach and leader, I've come to realize one of the keys to leading a successful life is changing our perceptions of situations by seeing them as opportunities to learn and to experience personal growth. By releasing the need to control things outside of ourselves and embracing them as learning opportunities, we begin to gain self-control.

CHAPTER 10

Dare to Dream

I believe the most important single thing beyond discipline and creativity is daring to dare.

Maya Angelou

At the beginning of the book, I told you a lot about my early life, about how little we had and how hard my parents had to work just to get by. While I still have concerns about money and getting the bills paid, like almost everyone else, sometimes when I look back at how I was raised in East Liverpool, I can't help but feel blessed. I'm far from rich, but I've still come a long, long way. The ramshackle house with a leaky roof on a treacherous dirt road has been replaced by a lovely home in a suburb, made even lovelier by Carolyn's impeccable taste as an interior designer.

But that journey was only possible because of a certain something that I believe sits somewhere between our imagination and our potential, which I'll call *our dreams*.

If I strip it down, I've had two fundamental dreams — both of which felt entirely out of reach at different points in my life. One was the dream of being a father and husband, and the other was the dream of being a coach.

When I was a college student spending my time womanizing and getting high, the very last thing I ever imagined I would achieve was husband and fatherhood status. It seemed as far away from me then as the moon, and my daily behavior only served to push it farther away. But since I never stopped dreaming about the family life I wanted, I was able to flip a switch — one that finally gave my wife, Carolyn, the sacred space she deserved in my life. By giving her the respect and place she warranted on the stage of my life, I was able to create what I always knew would be my greatest accomplishment, namely, my family.

Similarly, when I was fifteen years into my career at ConAgra, the last thing I would have imagined was not only that one day I'd be a high school basketball coach but also that *USA Today* would name me coach of the year after St. Vincent-St. Mary won the national championship.

Needless to say, my life journey felt like a miracle of epic proportions to me. Sure, a certain amount of serendipity and circumstantial lining up had to happen for this miracle to unfold. But the one ingredient that truly made it possible was the fact that I allowed myself to dream of it.

Now when we talk about dreams, we usually think about the stuff that happens when we're asleep. But the kind of dreams I'm talking about are the dreams in our lives that we *wake up* to, those dreams that come to us as revelations of our selves. This is what happened to me when I made the choice to walk away from corporate America. I made the choice to stop going through the motions each day and instead found a way to wake up to my dream.

But these things typically don't happen overnight, nor do they happen on their own. If your dreams don't just one day magically land into your lap, how are you supposed to access them? Or more simply, what does it take to make one's dreams come true?

In my experience, it begins with listening to the whispers of our heart, which happens when we unplug from the world around us and from the tyranny of urgency and simply listen to the Creator. Call it meditation, call it prayer, call it whatever you will — but I believe a lot of the answers we seek reveal themselves during this special and crucial time alone with God.

When I speak of the heart, I am referring to our unconscious mind, this place of great mystery but also great truth. In some ways, it's much more advanced than the conscious mind because it knows more than we consciously know. We have to be able to tap into this great mystery and find a way to articulate its directions. As for me, when I made the choice to switch gears professionally, you might say I heard God's voice — a quiet voice, one that emanated from stillness and serenity — which could only come from a deep place within my heart.

So when I did decide to leave, my mind was flooded not with doubt but with a flurry of ideas and possibilities as to how to craft my new plan. And with that certainty and clarity, I was able to leave my job of twenty-five years and begin a walk of faith.

I knew that if I didn't change something in my life radically, if I didn't show the courage to be my most authentic self, things would only get worse. I knew I was taking a monumental risk in voluntarily walking away from the comfort of stability, and that this "faith walk" would demand not only my utmost trust in God but also a ton of hard work.

God is the giver and keeper of our dreams. It is through our interaction with Him that we are able to realize our dreams. It is like a dance between us and God. In this dynamic relationship with God, sometimes we lead the dance with our effort and attitude. Then God leads through His divine providence (some call it coincidence or the stars being aligned or even a miracle). It's what happens when that unexplainable thing occurs on our journey. But the truth is that the Creator is active in our dance, and when those unexplainable things fall into place that open doors or remove obstacles or help us see things more clearly, we need to acknowledge God's hand in our walk. Know that He is leading you through those moments in your dance.

As I began to find my way when I left the security of corporate America, God's providence in those unexplainable moments was clear, and the more I acknowledged His work, the more I began to see His movements.

In December 2003, I went to Dru's first college game. The University of Akron was playing the Cincinnati Bearcats, coached by Bob Huggins. The Cincinnati roster included four players from Texas and just one from Ohio. This bothered me because St. Vincent-St. Mary had just won the *USA Today* national championship, and I didn't think any state had better players than Ohio. I asked someone who wrote for a recruiting service why Ohio was so underrepresented on the Cincinnati bench. He explained that the NCAA rule at the time only allowed Division I coaches to evaluate players during the month of April in events sanctioned by the state governing body for high school athletics. The athletic association in Texas sanctioned April tournaments, while the Ohio High School Athletic Association (OHSAA) didn't. As a result, I felt Ohio was being underrecruited, and athletes from Texas were better represented on Division I college rosters. I asked him what it would take to get the OHSAA to approve an event, to which he said, laughing, "A politician."

Not knowing how to navigate the political arena but wanting to give Ohio basketball players a better chance to play Division I basketball, I sought help to bring an annual tournament to Ohio. By the fall of 2005, I had the city of Akron's support, along with that of some business leaders, but I still didn't have someone with political clout to get the ball rolling.

God began to lead in our dance when Larry Long, a young man from (of all places) East Liverpool, my hometown, contacted me about insurance, of all things. I had watched Larry's dad play football as a kid, just as Larry had watched me. Larry asked me about my plans since I was no longer working for ConAgra. I shared that I wanted to create a travel team basketball event to showcase Ohio high school players but that I needed the OHSAA to sanction the event, which would allow Division I coaches to attend. I'll never forget the excitement in Larry's voice when he said, "Dru, the Speaker pro tempore of the Ohio House of Representatives lives in East Liverpool. His name is Chuck Blasdel." He went on to explain that not only did he represent East Liverpool, but he had grown up in Akron, and his dad was a longtime girls basketball coach at Akron's Central-Hower High School. Larry didn't stop there. He also said that Chuck Blasdel was planning to run for the soon to be vacated U.S. House of Representatives seat and was having a cookout the coming weekend to announce his candidacy. Larry suggested I go with him, and he would introduce me to Chuck.

I went to the cookout, and things happened faster than I ever imagined they could. Not only did I meet Chuck, but when I explained how I wanted to showcase Ohio basketball players, he immediately asked his aide to set up a meeting with Dan Ross, the commissioner of the OHSAA.

Chuck's aide called me that Monday to give me the details of a meeting with the commissioner in Columbus. Some may call it a coincidence, but I see it as God at work. In fact, God had only begun. He continued to lead in our dance. The meeting took place in October 2005 in the offices of Representative Blasdel. I passionately explained to Commissioner Ross how important NCAA-sanctioned travel team tournaments are in the recruiting process. The commissioner listened intently and then posed the question, "Dru, do you have the support of the Ohio High School Basketball Coaches Association?" I said I didn't, and he said that without their support there was no way he could sanction the event. The meeting adjourned with the firm awareness that I needed to get the coaches association on board before any idea of sanctioning a travel team tournament could proceed.

We left the conference room, and Representative Blasdel invited us into his office. As we sat down, Chuck asked if there was any way I could get the coaches association's support. God continued to lead. I told Chuck I had the answer, and I knew it was only God's hand. Nike had sent me to work Michael Jordan's Basketball Camp in the summer of 2004. I went to learn from George Raveling, a former college basketball coach who was the head of Nike's basketball marketing, about how to plan and execute a basketball camp, as I was to be a partner with George on a camp for Bron. I understood clearly in Representative Blasdel's office that while Nike wanted me to learn the camp business, the Lord had me there for one reason and one reason only — to meet Norm Persin. Norm was a veteran Ohio high school basketball coach and a former president of the coaches association. Norm and I hit it off that summer, and I knew if anyone could get the coaches association to support my idea, it was Norm.

Norm agreed with what I was trying to do and said, "I'm no longer president of the association, but the leadership tends to listen to me." He said the next meeting was in November, and he'd let me know their decision. A few weeks later, Norm called and said the answer was yes! The coaches association supported my idea for a sanctioned travel team event, which at the time was the first sanctioned event in the Midwest. Once the coaches were on board, Commissioner Ross gave his support, and we received our formal letter sanctioning our event on January 2, 2006. God then stepped back and gave me the lead.

The King James Shooting Stars Classic just finished its ninth year. We have grown from an amazing 318 teams the first year — *amazing* because we were able to put it together in three months — to an event that consistently has more than 500 teams. More than two million dollars is poured into the local economy, and I've been given a business where I make twice as much as I did in my sales job.

Looking back, I don't regret those years in corporate America because it gave me an understanding of business. I learned a lot — how to handle budgets, how marketing works, and how to work with people. I wouldn't have been able to run the events I now run without those experiences.

I know that God honors effort. Ten years ago, I never would have imagined I'd be doing what I'm doing. I work on planning a tournament for nine months, for which the income starts coming in during March and April. We're currently up to five events and are forming partnerships. It's not only challenging but also deeply rewarding. I wake up each morning excited about the day, eager to solve problems and face obstacles. I feel empowered, capable, and passionate — and because I use my brain, I know I'm doing what my heart wants.

Today I'm clear about my motivations — that I produce the events primarily so I can continue to coach. Because I now know with clarity that the coaching is what God wants — and not just so I can live out my dreams but also so I can be an example to young men. I am there to coach them, but they also get to see what I've been able to accomplish from a business point of view, so they learn to recognize a person can create great things if they work hard.

I'm also clear that I'm not coaching for the money. You can't be a high school coach if you're in it for the money. When people hear what I make at St. Vincent-St. Mary, they're shocked. Let's just say you couldn't live off the salary if you were a single guy with no one depending on you, let alone as the patriarch of an extended family. You don't coach high school basketball if you're in it for the money — but if you're in it for the right reasons, the money will follow. It might not be there right when you start, but it will eventually come.

By the way, I should mention how proud I am that my wife, Carolyn, took a similar faith walk in her own middle age. Growing up, she had always dreamed of being a designer but never pursued that passion after her family convinced her it was too risky a career choice. She earned a bachelor's degree in political science from the University of Pittsburgh. Over the years she tried her hand at other professions but never found anything that engaged and satisfied her like design. Finally, realizing that God had blessed her with a gift, she recently went back to school and is earning a degree in interior design. Even though she is somewhat older than most of her fellow students, she's thrown herself into her schoolwork and is positioned to graduate with honors. Her story is a true testament to the fact a person is always happiest when they grab the dream God has blessed them with.

A DREAM DEFERRED

"What happened to a dream deferred? Does it dry up like a raisin in the sun?"[*] This line from Langston Hughes's poem "Harlem" prompts me to share an experience I had just the other day. One of my former players had a very close relative murdered. I went to the wake to support him and his family. The outpouring from the community was massive. Cars were parked three and four blocks away in every direction. I saw a lot of young people I hadn't seen in a long time — former athletes who had dreamed of playing professionally, single mothers who had dreamed of college, young men who now sell drugs because they lacked marketable skills.

As I spoke to many of them, it saddened me to discover they had not fulfilled their dreams. They fell into lifestyles that were aging them quickly. They had lost the hope of ever realizing the dreams that had once captivated them as children.

But dreams, no matter how large or small or how intangible they may seem, can be rekindled with faith and effort. The universe is filled with endless possibilities. What may look impossible to the naked eye is still achievable if we can recognize positive opportunities in our lives that are presented daily and grasp hold of them.

Dreams have to be nurtured in order to grow. Sometimes this maturation process can take a long time to develop. There may be many bumps in the road, but we can't allow the bumps to cause us to give up. Admitting defeat is what I saw that day. Too many people give

---

[*] Langston Hughes, "Harlem," in *The Collected Works of Langston Hughes: The Poems, 1951 – 1967*, ed. Dolan Hubbard (Columbia: University of Missouri Press, 2001), 74.

up on their dreams and stop pursuing them when life throws them a curve. I believe we have to learn to persist through the obstacles. We have to believe as if everything depends on God and work as if everything depends on us.

MAGIC HAPPENS — IF YOU HELP IT

After Lord knows how many drills, workouts, practices, wins, losses, fights, arguments, attitude adjustments, and a thousand other travails, in 2003, the Fab Five's senior year, the Fighting Irish of St. Vincent-St. Mary were at last slated to play in the Division II State Championship game against Kettering Alter High School, which if they won would ensure them the honor of being national champions.

"You have the chance to go down as the greatest high school team in basketball history, which is a legacy that's going to be around long after you guys are gone," I said as we huddled as a group in the locker room before the game, for what might have been our last time together. "We're taking it full circle, fellas." I'll never forget how their heads were bowed toward their feet, an air of solemnity hanging thick in the air, hearts pumped with adrenaline, nostalgia, and the desire to finish what we started so many years ago.

"This all started in a little gym with a linoleum floor on Maple Street at the local Salvation Army," I said. "All the travel we've done from the time you guys were eleven years old, all the way across the country, through high school, will culminate when that bus pulls up tomorrow — where? On Maple Street. And the only question right now is, *When you get off that bus tomorrow, will you get off victorious?*"

As wound up as I was for the game, I felt a surge of pride watching my players make their way onto the court, all of them linked at the arms like a cluster of closeness. They had a ritual before each game where they created a formation of two lines, and one by one, each player ran through the center of the two lines, giving low fives to his teammates and emerging at the other end to bump chests with the guy who had gone before him, as a kind of symbolic acknowledgment of their individual significance — but even more so, of their unity as a team. It was their way of establishing and honoring their brotherhood.

But no matter how motivated and determined the boys were, Kettering Alter was not messing around either. In fact, they came into the game with a well-planned strategy to neutralize our speed and athleticism. Every time they got the ball, instead of looking for a shot they patiently passed the ball around the perimeter, passing and cutting until someone would be out of position and frustrated. Once we were off-balance and out of sorts, they attacked, beating us for easy layups. One of their guards, Doug Penno, was particularly damaging, scoring 9 points in the first half. That might not sound like much, but at halftime Kettering was leading 19 – 14. That's right, our high-flying team, poised to win a national championship, had managed only 14 points in the first half. Things weren't looking good. And I knew going into the locker room, we were all thinking the same thing: *We simply cannot lose in the championship game two years in a row.* Which is exactly what you should *not* be thinking during halftime of a close game.

"Fellas," I said once we'd all gathered together, "it's not about the X's and O's right now. I want you to try for just a minute to grasp this thing. Grasp the opportunity you've been given. Look around the room, guys. Some of these guys — Dru, Bron, Sian, Romeo, Willie — you'll never play another game of basketball together again. Let's be real about this. To be where you guys are is a blessing you guys will only understand later in life. This will probably be the last game I coach with some of you guys. There have been a lot of great times and tons of great memories. And I'm going to cherish them. So let's do this. Let's end this thing the right way."

I walked to the blackboard to review the strategy and something told me to stop. I turned to look at them. "Forget all this stuff. It's not about strategy right now; it's about what's inside here," I said as I placed the palm of my hand on my chest.

As a team, we had to prove what was in our hearts. It was their last chance to do what they had been dreaming about since the fifth grade, winning a national championship. And they did.

Our comeback started with a defensive switch, as I put Dru on Penno and told him to make defense his only priority in the second half. "I don't care if you score another point," I said. "Just shut him down."

The switch worked, and with their top scorer neutralized, Kettering's offense began to lose its rhythm. And on the offensive end, we began to finally find ours. With Bron finding open teammates, we slowly got back in the game and even opened up a ten-point lead. But championship games are rarely blowouts, and this game proved to be no exception. Kettering clawed its way back into the game and even launched a three-point shot in an attempt to tie it in the waning seconds. They missed, and we were champs.

The sound of that buzzer was the sound not only of our monumental victory against a particularly tough opponent but also of a dream coming into fruition at last. We all ran out onto that court in a huddle of celebratory relief, our emotions ranging from euphoria to nostalgia. I had so many things I wanted to say, so many scenes I wanted to etch into my memory right there and then, to capture forever. But all we could do was laugh and cry and hold each other and throw our arms in the air and relish the moment.

When I went to hug Dru, I held him close, and in his ear, I whispered, "Don't ever give up on your dream; look at me." My message was twofold. First, I didn't want him to find himself in midlife wondering where he went wrong. I wanted my son, and all my kids, to learn from my experiences and get it right from the start. And second, as I hugged him that day, I wanted him to know that dreams do come true. That my journey in finding my purpose, my way back to that childhood desire to become a coach, did take place, that I had really been a football man who embraced basketball to help make my son's dream happen. Through me stepping up to the plate that day at the community center in Akron when the rec league director told me Dru could play if I coached, we shared a dream, and as hard as that was sometimes, it was also a beautiful thing.

After the game, the team came home to a welcoming committee of massive crowds swarming the streets, camera crews, and handmade signs singing their praises. People were clapping and cheering and videotaping, as if something historic, something epic, was unfolding in our very own Akron. Even the mayor of Akron came and spoke at the school.

In the high school corridors, everyone was dancing and celebrating and hugging one another. There was a euphoria I'd never witnessed before. Kids were painting their faces green and spraying their hair green, all of it as a tribute to their beloved Fighting Irish, the team that never gave up on the dream. Yellow streamers hung from the ceiling, celebrating one giant party whose momentum seemed unstoppable.

And all of this because they — we — dared to dream.

I am a man of serious faith, yet I've learned over the years that faith alone will take us only so far. As Scripture puts it, "Faith by itself, if it is not accompanied by action, is dead" (James 2:17). While I had faith that I could not only survive but thrive outside of the comfortable confines of corporate America, faith was only realized because I put tremendous effort into becoming a basketball coach and using my talents to build a business around the sport of basketball. In this way, I not only dared to dream, but I also found a way to make my dreams come true on terms that made the most sense for me.

Ultimately, no matter who you are, how old you are, or how bad, hopeless, painful, or boring your life may seem at any given moment, you can always take action. And even though I keep saying this book isn't about basketball, I leave you with a metaphor from the sport: Think of each day of your life as the beginning of a game, with the strongly held conviction that every time the ball gets thrown into the air, anything is possible.

Anything.

ACKNOWLEDGMENTS

To Chris, thank you for believing in this project, at times more than I did. Your star is rising, and I'm grateful you have taken us along. To Monica, thank you for standing in the gap. Your work is much appreciated — more than words can say.

Special thanks to Kris Belman and Harvey Mason, two of the creative forces behind the the acclaimed documentary *More Than a Game*. Without the documentary and the publicity tour, this book wouldn't have happened.

To Margaret and Erin at WME Entertainment, thank you for all your hard work in making my dream come true.

To John Sloan and the entire Zondervan team, thank you for believing I had something worth saying. I can't tell you how humbled I am that you would take a chance on a high school coach.

To my mother, father, and sister, JoAnne, who have all gone on to be with the Lord. Everything begins with you three in my life. I couldn't have asked for better parents or a more inspiring big sister. We miss you.

Special thanks to my daughters, Ursula and India. You shared me with so many people and never complained. But always remember — I coached you two first.

Special thanks to my sons, Dru III and Cameron, and to Bron, Sian, Willie, Romeo, and all my players, who are like sons to me. Space doesn't allow me to name all of you, but know that I've enjoyed the time we've spent together. It has been my honor to be involved in your lives. I continue to encourage all of you to never give up on your dreams. To the parents of my players, it has been a great ride. Sometimes the road has been bumpy, but you believed in me enough to let me be a part of your sons' lives, and for that I am eternally grateful.

To my father-in-law and mother-in-law, Reverend Cleo and Mildred Brooks, thank you for your daughter, my wife, Carolyn. She is everything you said she would be. Your prayers and help over the years mean more than you will ever know.

To my sons-in-law, David and Corey, and my daughters-in-law, Lanae and Devin, you are great additions to the family. Thank you for making my children complete and for your hard work in helping make our tournament business what it is today.

To my spiritual leaders — Bishop Joey Johnson, words can't say how much you've impacted my life; Pastor Richard Walker, my friend and discipler, miles and life have put distance between us, but my walk would not be the same without you. Robert "Mac" McFarland, my spiritual journey began with you. You are and have been a great friend. Chuck Swindoll, John Maxwell, Charles Stanley, Deepak Chopra, your words have inspired me.

Special thanks to Kirk Linderman, Lee Cotton, James Tribble, Rick Bock, Percy Robinson, Brian Bachman, and the long list of travel team coaches. Your service to the kids touched by our program may go unnoticed by some, but your sacrifice will always be honored by me.

To Keith Dambrot and the STVM coaches I've had the privilege of sharing the sidelines with, thank you. We've done a great job building a dynasty that will not be forgotten. Brian Knight and Dr. Mike Magoline, I've said many times that you guys, the STVM training staff, are the reason I stay. Thank you for your selfless service not only to my athletes but to all the athletes at STVM. Lee Wolf and Jim Sansonetti, you both have made my job easier. Thank you for all you do. Thanks to the Piglia family for your support.

Special thanks to Aaron Bachman, Kevin McIntyre, and Tina

McIntyre. You make the King James tournaments successful. They wouldn't be what they are without you. You are always there for me, and I appreciate it.

To Mayor Don Plusquellic and the city of Akron's recreation department, thank you for your partnership and your help in making the King James Shooting Stars Classic the best travel team tournament in America.

To Patty Burdon and Ryan Thogmartin, your pictures capture the essence of STVM basketball. Thank you for your good work.

Last, but surely not least, thanks to the St. Vincent-St. Mary family for giving me a chance. I think we've done pretty good, I hope you do too.

MORE THAN A GAME: COACH DRU JOYCE II

Abridged excerpts from an interview by Michael Dequina, October 23, 2009, at www.themoviereport.com; used by permission of Michael Dequina, www.themoviereport.com.

MD: *Were you always a fan of the game of basketball?*

DJ: Growing up, I played basketball. I didn't play basketball in high school. Ninth grade was still part of junior high when I grew up years and years ago. When I was in junior high, I got cut from the ninth-grade basketball team. I wasn't great, but I was like, "Dang, they kept some guys …" Anyway, long story short, the next year I go to high school, and that coach [at the junior high] moved to the high school and became the junior varsity coach. I didn't have someone [at school] to encourage me, and my parents, especially my mother, weren't really into athletics. I was the only one in my family who was playing basketball; in my extended family, all of my cousins, everyone—we all played football. So because of [the junior high coach] going there and no one encouraging me to try out again, I just didn't play any more basketball other than pickup and intramurals when I got into college, and I played on a church league team while I was in high school. That was pretty much my basketball history.

MD: *So you played a lot of football, then.*

DJ: Yeah. That was the sport I grew up loving. I started at ten years old and played every year all the way through high school, and I went to college to play football. And honestly, I got to college and decided I wasn't going to play because it was a small Division III school. I didn't have to play, but it was one of those kinds of things why I really stress to my sons now to chase their dream and not give up on it, because I wish I had played in college. It's one of those things where you think back and say, "What if … ?"

MD: *And you went to Ohio University?*

DJ: My first year, I went to Ashland College; that's where I was going to play football. I was there for a year. I had come from a small town in Ohio, and Ashland was a little school, and it was just too much like high school and like being in the small town I grew up in, so I wanted to go someplace different. The next year, I transferred to Ohio University. I think Ashland had fifteen hundred students, and Ohio University had fifteen to seventeen thousand students, so it was much more to my liking as far as the college environment.

MD: What did you end up studying in college?

DJ: I studied business and economics. I was the first person in my family to go to [college], so I really didn't know what to do. I went out and interviewed, just trying to find a job. At first I was trying to find a job in banking, and they wanted guys who had a master's degree. So I got a job in consumer sales, and there were some things about it I liked: they gave you a car; you worked out of your home; you kind of made your own day, and I really enjoyed that. With sales, there's a lot of reward in that you know at the end of the day you either sold something or didn't, if it was a good day or a bad day. So I always responded to those kinds of things as far as who I am as a person.

MD: While you were in the thick of your career in sales, was coaching something in the back of your mind that you also wanted to pursue?

DJ: In the small town I came from, there were very few African-American role models, especially as professionals. When I was in high school, I had a coach—a young guy who had just graduated from college. He coached football and track and was a teacher, and I liked who he was and the lifestyle he led. I know he helped me; we talked a lot about things outside of just sports. So I had that desire [to coach] going into college, and once I stopped playing, that desire went away with my not playing because I was under the assumption that you go to school, you play the sport, then you graduate and become a coach because you had that experience in college.

MD: Was your first coaching experience for youth basketball teams in the Amateur Athletic Union?

DJ: Actually, my first coaching experience was when [son] Dru [Joyce III] was seven. In Akron, the rec leagues start at eight years old. Tryouts are in November, and the season starts in December/January. Dru didn't turn eight until January 29, but he was very skilled and wanted to play. We took him to a recreation center, and I told the coach, "Hey, he's really good, and he can play against these kids who are a little bit older; trust me, I know he can." The guy said, "We've already picked our teams, but here's what we'll do: I'll let him play, but you've got to coach the team, and we're going to take one player from each of the other teams [to form yours]." So I got my son, and then you can probably figure out who I got from all the other teams. I got the worst player from every other team. So that was my very first experience with coaching. That season, we played ten games and won one and lost nine. The next year, I got a promotion at work, and Dru was eight, turning nine, and the [coach] whose team had been very good wanted him to come and play on his team. So I let Dru play with his team, but whenever I could, I came to practice and helped out, but I was traveling more at that point. It was a time when I was getting some recognition. We were doing a lot of focus groups. So I was flying to our corporate headquarters in California or to meetings in New York or elsewhere. Then going into that next year, Dru is in fourth grade—he's nine turning ten and playing rec ball. I'm still not coaching; I'm just kind of helping out. A guy comes into the rec center, and he's scouting the kids. He looked out of place because this rec center is in an African-American community, and there's a young white guy sitting in the stands taking notes. After Dru's game is over, the scout comes over and says, "Hey, I really like how your son plays; I have a fifth-grade travel team I'm putting together and maybe he can try out." Dru tries out as a fourth grader, and he makes the team. Dru had played against LeBron [James] that rec season, and I knew about LeBron because I knew the coach of his team really well. That's when I went to Frankie Walker and asked him to put me in touch with LeBron and LeBron's mother. So I asked LeBron to be a part of that team at the end of their fourth-grade year. In travel basketball, the parents pool their money to get into tournaments, and that year, there was a national championship tournament in Florida the team wanted to go to. The coach said they didn't have enough money to go, so a couple of families that wanted their sons to have this experience left our team. We didn't have enough players, so the team fell apart after a few practices. Then that next fall, I got a phone call from some of the parents, and they said, "You were at practice most of the time. Why don't you coach the team?" At this point, I was still traveling, but all of it was local; I was just calling on the major accounts in Northeast Ohio.

MD: *So now you had more time to devote to this coaching "side gig."*

DJ: Yeah, exactly. I was still playing pickup basketball, and every Saturday morning, the guys from my church would get together. So I had a feel for the game; I enjoyed watching it. But when I started coaching, I felt like, "Wow, I want Dru to learn this thing and learn it right." So I did two things. I started reading books about basketball. And I talked to a high school basketball coach who went to my church, and I said, "Hey, Dru really likes this game, and he's doing well. What should I do?" He said, "Put him in the camps, and you'll see what I'm talking about." So I put Dru in any camp that came around, and I sat through all the camps I could make and tried to pick up coaching tips. That's kind of how we got started—him playing and me coaching.

MD: *So as far as the core group of four goes, LeBron joined Dru first?*

DJ: LeBron was there in fifth grade, and in December of their fifth-grade year, we started practicing [as a team]. Sian [Cotton] and Dru were fifth graders, and the rest of the team was made up of sixth graders. In January, February, and March, we started playing travel tournaments around the area.

MD: *And Willie [McGee] came in later, moving to Akron from Chicago?*

DJ: Willie had already moved from Chicago by then; he was living with his brother. Actually—this is how small Akron is—when Willie was nine years old, Dru's team played LeBron's team in the rec league championship game, and Willie was on LeBron's team.

MD: *When did you start getting formal school coaching jobs? You were on staff at Buchtel High School before the four went to high school?*

DJ: Our travel team was doing really well. A man named Chris Marciniak helped sponsor the team—that's when we got the name Shooting Stars—and he did basketball camps around the area. At the 11-and-under [age bracket] I started coaching the travel team, and he bought us uniforms. Whenever he did a clinic, I'd be one of the coaches there and take Dru with me. One day, Chris said, "Hey, I got a couple of seventh graders I want to add to your team." One was the grandson of Sam Salem, who was a great player at the University of Akron in the late 1940s. Sam knew Harvey Sims, the head coach at Buchtel High School, the reigning city series champ. Sam told Harvey about me as a coach. So the summer before [the guys] were going into seventh grade, Harvey invited me to go to his basketball camp at Buchtel with my kids. For the sixth- to seventh-grade year, I kept my relationship with Harvey going, and during their eighth-grade year, the kids and I talked about them going to Buchtel because they wanted to go to school together, and Buchtel was the obvious choice. It was pretty well-known that we intended to take our kids to Buchtel, so Harvey asked me to join the coaching staff. But Dru never got a real good feel for [Buchtel]. He felt they thought he was too little and wouldn't give him a fair shot. After the third game of the eighth-grade season, he said, "Dad, you know what, I've thought about this. I'm not going to Buchtel. I want to go to St. V." He said, "At St. Vincent-St. Mary, Coach [Keith] Dambrot isn't going to look at my size; he's going to give me a chance to play." And I said, "Dru, everything's in place; what do you mean? I'm on the staff; we've got all this stuff going for us. Why would you want to do this?" He said, "Dad, I can see how they look at me." And he was right. I saw it, but I felt Dru was good enough, and he was going to show them. But Dru didn't think they'd even give him a chance to show them.

MD: *How did your and Dru's relationship with Coach Keith Dambrot come about?*

DJ: [Dru] started a relationship with Coach Dambrot in seventh grade. I used to take him on Sunday nights to the Jewish community center where Coach Dambrot was doing a clinic. That year, Keith was named head coach of St. Vincent-St. Mary High School; while Dru was in eighth grade, he was the first-year coach at St. V.

MD: *Then you ended up getting a coaching staff position at St. V. under Coach Dambrot.*

DJ: Yeah. Keith is very knowledgeable about basketball. We were trying to be the best team we could be, so I was bending his ear, trying to find out everything he knew about basketball. We had built this relationship, and when Keith got the job and the kids were coming [to St. V.], he asked me and Coach Cotton [Sian's dad] to be part of his staff as volunteers. So we said yes.

MD: *What was it like working under Coach Dambrot, as he has a reputation for being a bit fiery, to put it mildly?*

DJ: It was different because of his fiery nature. But the bottom line is he loves basketball, and he cared about the kids. We have different styles to some degree; I can get excited when I need to. But it was great because I learned a whole lot those two years under Coach Dambrot, who was teaching the kids what he had taught as a Division I college coach at Central Michigan. So what the kids were learning I was learning with them; he helped them, and he helped me. Most of what we do today at St. Vincent-St. Mary hasn't changed a whole lot [from Dambrot's system]. I'm better at it [than in the early years], but we haven't changed because it's just great basketball. The one thing college coaches say to me about our kids who go on to play in college is that they are prepared; they're ready to play. They have a good understanding of how the game is played.

MD: *And you had your misgivings about taking over as head coach when Coach Dambrot left.*

DJ: Yeah. I didn't want to mess it up. [The team] had won two state championships; they had a chance to win four in a row, and no one's ever done that in the state of Ohio. The big thing was Keith and I had put the schedule together for that junior season, and we laughed about it. This was before he accepted the job at the University of Akron. He said, "We might be the first team to go 10 and 10 in the regular season and win a state championship," because we had highly ranked teams from all over the country coming to the University of Akron to play us, and the schedule the first two years was nothing compared to what it was that junior year. So I recognized all that. The other thing is that the school's enrollment had grown, and we were going from Division III to Division II, the second largest division in the state of Ohio, so our tournament path would be much tougher than we'd ever had. So naturally I was a little hesitant. I knew at some point I was going to become a high school head coach. I just didn't think it would be then. [When I was offered the job], my wife said, "Dru, how could you say no? This is God's way of honoring all you've done for those boys." I realized in that moment it was about the opportunity to be involved with my son and the guys I'd been involved with since they were ten years old—and these other kids. It was an opportunity, so I ran with it.

MD: *It was already an unusual situation to jump into as a first-time head coach with the tough schedule, and then on top of it there was the unforeseen thing, which was LeBron's* Sports Illustrated *cover.*

DJ: Oh, my goodness, yes. You know, I was happy for LeBron, because I saw the kid grow and I know how hard he worked. It just took us to a level where I had no clue of what to do. I mean, who do you ask? That was tough, honestly, not knowing what to do, where to go, how to handle it. So I did what I thought was best and tried to manage it, but it was kind of overwhelming.

MD: Where did you think you fell short as a coach that season?

DJ: It was in reining in their emotions. In that championship game, there was a lot of pressure on the kids to win, but the thing was just growing so fast that I didn't know how to rein it in. We constantly had fifteen to twenty people hanging around at practice. Media everywhere. I just think my shortcoming was I didn't keep the guys focused. We were 23 and 3 going into the championship game [against Roger Bacon], and the guys allowed their success to go to their heads. And then [the morning of the game], LeBron got back spasms. We took him to Ohio State, and they gave him electric shocks to ease the muscles, but by game time the spasms had come back, so I had to make a decision. Do I let him play and hope he can work through them, or do I sit him and try to stretch him and keep him warm and see if I can bring him in later in the game? I chose to play him, and early on, for about the first two quarters, he didn't play well, and we made some mistakes. But Roger Bacon was a very good team, and they won the game.

MD: You guys had been fortunate to have a winning season under that pressure, but it seemed all that had been boiling underneath finally exploded at the least convenient moment for you guys.

DJ: Honestly, it was best it happened the way it did because it refocused the guys, and it refocused me to an extent. I was really caught up in the pressure of winning and losing. We had a motto when we started years ago with basketball, and it was, "Teach them how to play, and the winning will take care of itself." The other thing we stressed was that we wanted to use basketball to teach life skills. And I felt like I had lost that during that season; I wasn't helping them grow into adulthood. That loss helped me and the guys refocus, and that's why we had the success we did that senior year. I was concentrating on why I believe God put me in the position. When you consider the team we had, and the fact that other coaches with much more coaching experience were interviewing for the job and I got it, I knew God placed me there for a reason. I believed it in my heart because I knew these kids, and I knew they would play hard for me. But more than that, I knew I had to help them become men. That's what we always talked about—we want you to use basketball to help you become a productive member of society. The sport can't make you that, but you can use the sport to help get you there. We wanted to refocus on our core values. I'm always reading, and a Christian coach in a Division II school in Oregon had seven principles we stressed from that point on: unity, discipline, thankfulness, servanthood, passion, integrity, and humility.

MD: *When did Kris Belman [producer of* More Than a Game*] approach you to start filming the team, and how did that arrangement come about?*

DJ: It was their senior year, and we were getting ready to start the season. In early December, Kris contacted the school and got in touch with Patty Burdon, our public relations director. Patty introduced him to me and said, "Dru, this is Kris Belman; he's from Akron. He went to a rival high school—Walsh High School, one of our biggest rivals—but he's in school in California, and he wants to use you guys in a short documentary film for a class assignment." Though we had closed practices to the media and parents, Kris was from Akron. He wanted to do something I thought was innocent, and he didn't have ulterior motives. So I felt like, "Hey, I'm going to give him a shot. It's only going to be a few days—a couple of practices and a game, maybe. Then he can do his documentary." That's how I presented it to the kids, but Kris just kept on coming back. He was good about it because to this day I don't remember him ever being in the way. And once the guys warmed up to him—once those guys let you in—you're good. And they let him in.

MD: *Was it surprising that you ended up becoming the unifying figure to the piece?*

DJ: It's not been put to me that way; people have said different things about my role. Those are kind words if that's what you believe. I just know I definitely had a role. I recognize it's a sacred position you're given as a coach. And every day I recognize it even more, that the impact you can have on young lives is phenomenal. You need to honor and respect it, and to see that I've had that impact, I'm very thankful I was given the opportunity because it's nothing really about me. I didn't have a great coaching résumé. I've worked with kids; I've been in youth ministry at our church. But I was given the opportunity, and I'm thankful for it.

MD: *What do you hope viewers take away from the film?*

DJ: Dreams come true—not just [for] kids—if you're willing to take a risk. I left my job to do basketball, and I've been on a faith walk since that day. Every morning now, I get up and I'm excited about the day. When I got into consumer sales after leaving college, I was excited. But over the years, the job changed; it wasn't as rewarding, and my heart was no longer in it. I realized my dream at forty-nine years old, and that doesn't happen often. And Kris realized his dream to make a movie. Keith Dambrot realized his dream to get back into college basketball. So [the film is] just about dreams, and if you hold on to them and work at them, they can come true. It's also about friendship. When you've got friends who value you, it can mean the world in your development. I think those guys valued each other and held each other up, and it's meant great things for them. And you've got to recognize the struggle in life too, that everything isn't going to go your way. You've got to be resilient, to hold on to the dream because it's so easy to give up on your dream.

Beyond Championships Teen Edition: A Playbook for Winning at Life

Coach Dru Joyce II with Chris Morrow

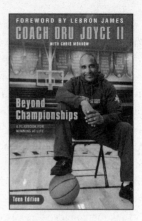

In *Beyond Championships Teen Edition*, Coach Dru Joyce II, high school coach of LeBron James, lays out the steps teens can follow to become winners on and off the court. Much more than a sports book, *Beyond Championships Teen Edition* is a blueprint for anyone looking to make better choices and reach their full potential. The book speaks to athletes aspiring to emulate LeBron's success, as well as to anyone who feels either uninspired or unable to change the direction of their lives.

Available in stores and online!

ZONDERVAN®
.com

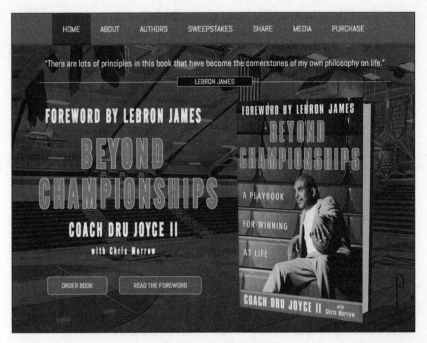

To watch an exclusive video and read articles and interviews with Coach Dru Joyce, check out the Beyond Championships website at www.beyondchampionships.com.

Welcome to the Northeast Ohio Basketball Association

For more information about the Northeast Ohio Basketball Association and to register for the King James Shooting Classic, visit the association's website at www.neobasketball.com.

Follow the King James Shooting Star travel teams, part of Nike grassroots basketball, by going to www.kingjamesshootingstars.com.